YUGOSLAVIA

Welcome to Yugoslavia

Sylvie Nickels

Collins
Glasgow and London

Cover Photographs
Van Phillips: Lake Bohinj (top), Ploče beach, Dubrovnik (l.),
Plitvice lakes (rt), Girl from Čilipi (btm)

Photographs
J. Allan Cash Ltd.
pp. 10, 29, 37, 44(l.), 46, 51, 59, 60, 62(l.), 65(btm), 84(btm)

Robert Harding Associates
p. 77

Van Phillips
pp. 15, 18, 32, 34, 35, 42, 43, 45, 47, 50, 52, 70, 72(btm), 73, 80(l.) 81(top),
82, 83(btm), 84(top)

Picturepoint Ltd.
pp. 22, 28, 54, 62(rt), 63, 65(top), 72(top), 74(btm), 75, 80 (top and btm rt),
81(btm), 85, 91

ZEFA
pp. 31, 40, 44(rt), 58, 61, 66, 74(top), 83(top), 86, 88(rt), 89, 90

Illustration
pp. 6–7 Peter Joyce

Town Plans
M. and R. Piggott

Regional Maps
Mike Shand, Kažia L. Kram, Iain Gerard

First published 1984
Copyright © text: Sylvie Nickels 1984
Copyright © maps: Wm. Collins, Sons & Co. Ltd.
Published by William Collins Sons and Company Limited
Printed in Great Britain

ISBN 0 00 447344 2

HOW TO USE THIS BOOK

The contents page of this book shows how the country is divided up into tourist regions (the six republics of Yugoslavia). The book is in two main sections: general information and gazetteer. The latter is arranged in the tourist regions with an introduction and a regional map (detail below left). There are also plans of main cities (detail below right). All main entries listed in the gazetteer are shown on the regional maps. Places to visit and leisure facilities available in each region are indicated by symbols. Main roads, railways and airports are shown on the maps.

Regional Maps

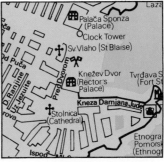

Town Plans

🏛	Museum/gallery	🎿	Winter sports
✝	Church/monastery	🚶	Walking/hiking
🕌	Mosque	🏊	Water sports
🏰	Castle/fortress	🛶	Canoeing/rafting
🏢	Interesting building	🌲	National park
m	Ancient site/monument		
✈	Airport		
▲	Climbing/mountainous		
⛵	Boating		
❀	Gardens		
♣	Park		
⋔	Spa		
🕳	Caves		
🦆	Birdlife		

🏛	Museum/gallery
✝	Church/monastery
🏰	Castle/fortress
🏢	Interesting building
m	Ancient site/monument
🎭	Theatre
📖	Library
⚜	Town hall
✉	Post office
ℹ	Information
♣	Park
❀	Garden
●	Railway station
🚌	Bus terminal
Ⓟ	Car park

metres	feet
1500	4921
1000	3281
400	1312
200	656
0	0

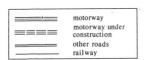

motorway
motorway under construction
other roads
railway

Scale 1:2,500,000

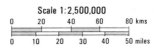

Every effort has been made to give you an up-to-date text but changes are constantly occurring and we will be grateful for any information about changes you may notice while travelling.

CONTENTS

Regions or Republics
1 Slovenia
(Slovenija)
2 Croatia
(Hrvatska)
3 Bosnia-Herzegovina
(Bosna I Hercegovina)
4 Serbia
(Srbija)
a Vojvodina
b Kosovo
5 Montenegro
(Crna Gora)
6 Macedonia
(Makedonija)

YUGOSLAVIA

About 80 per cent of Yugoslavia's visitors stay on the Adriatic coast. They may probe the interior on an excursion or two, but few of them can begin to guess at the variety of landscapes or the mosaic of cultural and historical influences that make this one of Europe's most fascinating – and at times infuriating – countries.

In a nutshell, the Socialist Federal Republic of Yugoslavia has frontiers with seven neighbouring countries, is composed of six very different republics, inhabited by five main Slav nationalities (and many minorities), speaking four principal languages, following three different religious faiths and using two alphabets. That all this has been moulded into one nation in the past few decades is little short of a miracle.

The six republics are Bosnia-Herzegovina, Croatia, Macedonia, Montenegro, Serbia (which includes the two autonomous regions of Kosovo and Vojvodina) and Slovenia. Between them they cover 255,804sq km/98,766sq mi of the Balkan peninsula, with a population of nearly 22½ million. The majority speak Serbo-Croat (comprising the slightly differing Serbian and Croatian languages) which varies substantially from Macedonian and Slovenian. Broadly speaking, the Roman Catholic faith is practised and the Roman alphabet used in the north and west; the Orthodox and Moslem faiths, along with the Cyrillic alphabet, predominate in the centre, south and east. (The reasons are explained in The Past and in the introductions to the republics in the gazetteer.) Such variations have led to an immensely rich diversity in the traditional architecture, music, costume, crafts and customs that make Yugoslavia seem like several countries rather than one.

In the north east, the plains fed by rivers such as the Danube and the Sava are a continuation of the great Hungarian plains, but more than 70 per cent of the country is composed of hills and mountain ranges and plateaus ribbed by glorious valleys and deep ravines scored by rivers tumbling, mainly northwards, on their way to join the Sava and the Danube. The greatest peaks are in the Julian Alps of Slovenia (Triglav at 2863m/9393ft is the highest) but down in the south several summits reach to over 2400m/8000ft in the neighbouring ranges of Macedonia, southern Serbia and Montenegro. Almost linking these mountain groups at opposite ends of the country is the Dinaric chain which runs parallel to the coast. A chief characteristic of many of the coastal and Slovenian mountains is their karst composition, a porous limestone given to the creation of fantastic caves and the oddly-behaving rivers that suddenly disappear underground to re-emerge considerable distances away.

Yugoslavia is rich in mineral and hydro-electric resources, has some of the highest-yielding agricultural land in Europe, and has diversified into every conceivable branch of manufacturing. In the space of four decades under the leadership of Josip Broz Tito, she emerged from the devastation and mass population losses of World War II to become a modern industrialized member of the family of nations, whose achievements and policy of non-alignment are respected by most. Economic recovery was achieved through discipline and grinding hard work; in the 1970s it snowballed almost too rapidly and Yugoslavia is now facing the realities of over-borrowing, over-diversification and a slump in productivity. Recent strict measures to put matters right, which affect the Yugoslavs rather than their visitors, have resulted in a series of currency devaluations and certain shortages, especially of imported goods, from time to time.

Yugoslavia's brand of Communism (or socialism as they prefer to call it) is unique. It is based on the principle of workers' self-management whereby, with few exceptions, every enterprise – from hotels, hospitals and schools to heavy industry – is owned and operated, not by the State, but by the people who work for it. This results in a degree of competition which comes as a great surprise to many foreigners. The principle is excellent; in practice, efficiency varies according to such usual human factors as know-how, diligence and self-interest. Decentralization has also arguably put too much responsibility at regional or local level. In addition, there is quite a thriving private sector – usually guest houses, restaurants,

shops or smallholdings – in which the maximum number of employees allowed (apart from family members) is normally five.

The Yugoslavs have had to pay a heavy price for the real, if at times shaky, miracle of political unity. Terrible things have been done to them and they have done terrible things to each other in the past. For a long time yet, there will be great variations in standards and efficiency, both of which improve progressively as you move from south east to north west. The tremendous upsurge in education, along with rapid modernization, has led to a major exodus from rural to urban areas since World War II, significantly affecting the very close family unit which has always been an intrinsic part of South Slav society. Yet the sons and daughters of farming and fishing folk readily leave their urban professions or trades at every opportunity to enjoy an interlude close to their rural roots.

These are a proud people, not always temperamentally suited to the streamlined service which makes for ideal tourism. Yet what sometimes seems like indifference, even surliness, is just as often counterbalanced by examples of great kindness, and a genuine and overwhelming hospitality.

THE PAST

The oldest traces of a developed society in Yugoslavia – and one of the oldest in Europe – are to be found at Lepenski Vir on the Danube, dating from as far back as 6000 BC. Since the 1960s, archaeological finds have changed much of the thinking on Europe's prehistory. Many experts now believe that the Bronze Age developed, not as a spread of skills brought from the East, but quite independently and much earlier than the dates so far attributed to several cultures, such as that of Vinča (2700–2000 BC) in the Danube basin close to Belgrade. These dates may now possibly be pushed back a further 1500 years or more.

The Danube has frequently played a leading role in Yugoslavia's evolution. The Celts followed its course downstream from their northern homelands, conquering and merging with the earliest named inhabitants of the region: the Illyrians. Later, when most of present-day Yugoslavia formed parts of the Roman provinces of Illyricum, Pannonia and Moesia, the Danube formed the boundary of the Roman Empire, acting as a buffer against the threat of the barbarians who eventually swarmed across. In AD 395, the Roman Empire was divided into East and West. When the South Slavs arrived in the 5th and 6th centuries, their future homeland was already under two very different spheres of influence: the eastern half (now Serbia, Macedonia, Montenegro and most of Bosnia-Herzegovina) was part of the Byzantine Empire, the western half (Croatia and Slovenia) part of the Holy Roman Empire.

Early South Slav society followed quite distinct lines, centred on the *zadruga*, the basic family unit or clan. Gradually the future pattern was set. In the north the Slovenes came increasingly under the influence of German, later Habsburg, rule. Much of Croatia came under Hungarian rule, eventually falling prey to Ottoman or Habsburg expansionism. Most of Dalmatia accepted Venetian sovereignty and enjoyed intermittent and varying degrees of independence until the fall of Venice in 1797, when it too passed to the Habsburgs. In Serbia things developed very differently. Under the Nemanjić kings, an independent medieval state grew strong and expanded to include most of present-day Serbia, Macedonia, Montenegro, Albania and half of Greece. Last and most powerful of this line of kings was Dušan who was poised to conquer the ailing Byzantine Empire. On his death, however, rivalries and squabbles eroded Serbian power. Too late was the rising threat of the Ottoman Turks recognized. The Serbs rallied their forces but suffered a bitter defeat at the Battle of Kosovo in 1389, marking the beginning of the dark ages for half the South Slav lands for nearly 500 years.

Those centuries were punctuated by uprisings between periods of uneasy quiet or oppression. Further details are given in the introductions to each republic, but the Serbs were the first to shake free during the 19th century, subsequently lending support to neighbouring regions, which resulted in a series of events that exploded into World War I (pp. 55, 67). The war over, the Austro-Hungarian Empire disappeared from the map of Europe and one of the many countries to replace it was the Kingdom of the Serbs, Croats and Slovenes – renamed Yugoslavia in 1928. The new state inherited enormous economic problems and growing disunity, notably between Serbs and Croats, under the autocratic rule of King Alexander. The increasingly popular Communist party was banned in 1921 and one of its most ardent followers, Josip Broz, the future Tito, was imprisoned from 1928–34. In the meantime the fascist Ustaše movement, supported by Mussolini, was also growing among exiled Croats. Alexander was assassinated in 1934 and succeeded by 11-year-old King Peter represented by three Regents, among them Prince Paul.

When World War II broke out in 1939, Yugoslavia was formally neutral but heavily dependent on German finance and bedevilled by a wavering foreign policy. A coup d'état on 27 March, 1941, overthrew the regency, declared Peter II of age (at 17 years) and replaced the government. In April, the Germans invaded, the government fled to London and Yugoslavia was fragmented, various parts going to Germany, Italy, Hungary or Bulgaria, while the remainder formed the independent state of Croatia under the pro-Nazi Ustaše.

Millions of Yugoslavs were stirred into revolt. Resistance was divided into two main factions: the Četniks, with a tendency to excessive Serbian nationalism and brutal habits, and the Communist-led Partisans under Tito whose almost legendary daring and dedication soon aroused the interest and then the active support of the Allies. The story of those times is magnificently described in Fitzroy Maclean's *Eastern Approaches*. After the war, elections in 1945 gave Tito massive support. Thereafter Yugoslavia developed her own brand of Communism which earned her expulsion from the Cominform in 1948 at a time when her economy was in tatters and her go-it-alone policies regarded with admiration but caution by the West.

Despite economic difficulties, she has kept doggedly to such fundamental principles as workers' self-management (p. 6) and the right of all her minority nationalities to decide their own affairs – not always easily accepted by some of the national majorities. Following Tito's death in 1980, the same principles continue to be developed under a system of rotating, collective and rather anonymous leadership devised by Tito himself to succeed him.

The seat of the Federal Republic is in Belgrade, but each of the six republics conducts its affairs – except those affecting the country as a whole – through its own Republic Assembly and Executive Council. All men and women over 18 years of age have the franchise which they can exercise both as individual citizens and through their places of work.

THE ARTS

The influences imposed by history have left Yugoslavia with a richness in variety of art forms and styles that would be difficult to match elsewhere in Europe.

Architecture The most significant pre-Slav monuments are Roman (listed where appropriate in the gazetteer). Medieval times left many Romanesque churches, mostly on the coast and islands, and the Orthodox monasteries that nestle in the mountain valleys of central and southern Serbia, Macedonia and Montenegro. Most of the Romanesque churches date from the 12th–13th centuries and were subsequently Gothicized. Interestingly, Romanesque influences are also marked in some of the earlier and more northerly and westerly of the Orthodox monasteries, while others bear the unmistakable hallmark of Byzantium. Within, the walls are veritable medieval art galleries in which the evolution of new and more humanistic art styles can clearly be seen. Some experts claim that this art foreshadowed the Italian Renaissance.

As a rough guide, the monasteries fall into three principal schools. Those of the Raška School of the 12th-13th centuries are usually divided into a narthex, naos with dome, and a chancel, its apse screened by an iconostasis. The frescoes are monumental, characterized by harmony of colour, boldness of stroke and, above all, a new sense of the dignity of man. The monasteries of the Central (or Kosmet and Macedonian) School of the 13th-14th centuries have a central square beneath a cupola, with four vaulted arms forming a cross and a supplementary cupola at each corner. The frescoes are crowded and narrative in aspect, the figures more dynamic, and in this group are the works of the Macedonian artists Mihajlo and Eutihije, among the few whose names are known to us. The Morava School, which centred on the Morava valley as Turkish pressure increased from the east, is mainly from the later 14th century. The buildings are often of an intricate brickwork design, with three apses giving a trefoil effect; the frescoes are usually quieter, more refined, with great attention to detail but less spontaneity.

Along the coast, Venetian Gothic predominates in all major secular buildings, usually with Renaissance adaptations and embellishments, or marked by the later heavier hand of Baroque. Most of the churches and palaces of inland Croatia and Slovenia are either Gothic or Baroque. If you are familiar with Central Europe, the influence of the Habsburg architects here is usually easy to recognize.

In the centre, east and especially the south of the country, mosques proliferate among the jumble of so-called Turkish houses which usually pre-date World War I. 'Turkish' is a misleading term since it is used to identify the period as much as the style of architecture, which is likely to have evolved from established domestic forms over several centuries. Typical houses are two-storeyed, wide-eaved, sometimes built round a courtyard and often with a broad verandah or overhanging balcony on one side of the upper storey. Windows are small and shuttered or partially latticed. The roofs of rounded tiles have a shallow slope. A distinct exception are the houses of Bosnia's mountains, with their roofs of dark wooden tiles steeply angled above white-washed walls. All this is in great contrast to the chalet-farms nestling in the lower folds of the Slovenian Alps.

Literature South Slav literature has its roots in folk ballads and poems passed on orally from one generation to the next; it resounds with daring deeds, many of them concerned with the struggle against the Turks. The best known in this respect are the *Ballads of Marko Kraljević* (p. 89), finally put on paper in the 19th century by Vuk Karadžić (1787–1864), a major figure in Yugoslav cultural life. He created the first Serbian dictionary and grammar and turned the language of the people into a literary medium.

In independent Ragusa (Dubrovnik) the arts flourished at an earlier date. The leading name was Marin Držić (1510–67) whose themes and style have been likened to those of Molière; one of his plays is usually featured in the Dubrovnik Festival, the best known being the comedy *Dundo Maroje* (Uncle Maroje). Elsewhere it was mainly in the 19th century that rising nationalism also found expression in a burst of literary activity. At one end of the country, the poet Franc Prešern (1800–49) was a leading figure in the national movement of Slovenia. At the other end, in Montenegro, the poet and prince-bishop Petar II Petrović-Njegoš (1813–51) dramatized historical incident to write tellingly of crises of conscience in the struggle against the Turks in *The Mountain Wreath.* The same struggle provided the theme for the Croatian writer Ivan Mažuranić (1814–90) in his *The Death of Smail-Aga.*

Probably the best and most balanced portrayal of life and times under the Turks is to be found in the works of Nobel Prize winner Ivo Andrić (1892–1975). His novel, *The Bridge on the Drina,* tells of ordinary Bosnian families over the centuries, from the building of the famous 16th-century bridge at Višegrad (p. 59) to the beginning of World War I. In contrast, *The Return of Philip Latinovicz,* by the Croatian writer Miroslav Krleža (1893–1981), is concerned with the decadence of society, a frequent theme between the two World Wars. Short stories by 20th-century Yugoslav writers can also be read in English in the collections translated by Dr. Svetozar Koljević.

Sculpture Some of the earliest examples of sculpture in Europe have been found on Yugoslav soil (Lepenski Vir, p. 73), and beautiful figurines from prehistoric cultures may be seen in the museums of the main cities. In historic times, the names of local families of stonemasons or master sculptors (Aleši, Andrijić, Buvina, Dalmatinac, Radovan) were perpetuated in some superb embellishments on Romanesque and Gothic churches and cathedrals, especially on the coast. In modern times, Ivan Meštrović (1883–1962) has achieved world renown as a sculptor. Two museums (in Split and Zagreb) focus on his work, but you will find examples all over Yugoslavia and abroad. Almost as famous is Antun Augustinčić. Among Yugoslavia's many war monuments there is a number of fine imaginative works by other sculptors.

Painting Apart from the remarkable contributions of the often anonymous fresco painters of the medieval monasteries (see Architecture above), Yugoslavia has produced no early artists of international stature. An interesting 20th-century development, however, has been the growth of several naive schools of painting, encouraged originally by the Croatian artist Krsto Hegedušić who discovered the talents of Ivan Generalić, a farming lad in the village of Hlebine. The Hlebine School of the 1930s has since been followed by others in Croatia and Serbia, especially in the flat Danubian plains (p. 72). Museums in Zagreb and Svetozarevo especially provide a good introduction to the vivid colours and simple forms with which these artists capture the essence of rural life and the seasons.

Folklore (See also pp. 21, 22.) Music and dance were the chief forms of entertainment until quite recent times and still feature strongly in festivals of all kinds. Both vary enormously from region to region, some concerned with religious or seasonal celebrations, and others rooted in far older fertility rites. The most common dance, the *kolo*, is a group dance not unlike the reel and the variations are legion. The greatest variety and most complex dances come from the republics of Serbia and Macedonia.

The one-stringed *gusle*, producing a rather mournful sound, is the best known of the traditional instruments, but there are also many wind instruments, which differ according to region, several varieties of mandolin, bagpipes and often a bass drum to give a regular beat. The actual harmonies produced by these instruments are as varied as everything else

in Yugoslavia – from the jolly tempo of the Slovene mountain villages and the nostalgic lilt of the Dalmatian fishermen's ballads to the haunting strains further east and south; and to these can be added the themes and melodies of Yugoslavia's many minority nationalities. A series of choral rhapsodies called *Rukoveti* (Bunch of Flowers) by the Serbian composer Stevan Mokranjac (1856–1914) draws on this rich store of folk melodies.

The ancient Orthodox tradition of the *slava* celebration is still quite widely practised, with feasting and dancing which may go on for a day or two (it used to be longer). This is in honour of the family's patron saint, though it may involve an entire village where every family has its *slava* on the same day.

Peasant wedding, Ljubljana

PAPERWORK

(See also If you are Motoring, p. 15.)

Passports A valid passport is required by all travellers to Yugoslavia. A British Visitor's Passport is also accepted, though holders will need to obtain a Tourist Pass (nominal fee, valid 30 days) at the frontier. A visa is not necessary for British nationals, but is required by citizens of some other countries including the United States, Canada, Australia and New Zealand; it is available from Yugoslav embassies and consulates abroad or at the frontier. For details of how to obtain a passport, UK citizens should get a passport application form from any main post office, and US citizens should apply to their nearest Passport Agency.

Health and Insurance (For emergency numbers, see p. 25.) There are no special health requirements for entering Yugoslavia. Their National Health Service is similar to that of the UK, and British citizens are entitled to free treatment at institutions forming part of that service.

You will need to produce your British passport and apply for exemption from payment at the time medical attention is required to avoid misunderstanding. You may have to pay the cost of certain medicines or drugs. If you are taking regular prescribed drugs, make sure you have an ample supply with you. Emergency treatment is always provided free, but in other cases the citizens of most other countries will need to pay for medical services and are advised to take out the appropriate insurance.

If you do not have your own favourite insurance company, both health and baggage insurance can be arranged through most travel firms, but read all the small print carefully to be quite sure you are getting the cover you want.

Yugoslavs are basically a very honest people, but there is no point in taking risks. Any loss or theft should be reported to the police and a copy of the report obtained to satisfy your insurers.

CUSTOMS

The following may be brought into Yugoslavia duty free on oral declaration: 200 cigarettes, 50 cigars or 250 grammes of tobacco; a bottle of wine; one litre of spirits; quarter litre of eau de cologne; small quantity of perfume; food required for the journey; two photographic cameras with 12 plates or five rolls of film; one small cine camera with two rolls of film; a pair of binoculars; a portable musical instrument, tape recorder, radio, TV set or typewriter; electronic pocket calculator; camping equipment; bicycle or sports boat with or without motor; one set of equipment per sport, *eg* fishing tackle, hunting weapon with 50 bullets, a pair of skis, two tennis rackets, *etc.* All items, except comestibles, must be re-exported.

Dogs and cats brought into Yugoslavia must be accompanied by a certificate stating that they have been vaccinated against **rabies** not less than 15 days or more than six months prior to date of entry.

The UK totally prohibits the importation of animals (including domestic pets) except under licence. One of the conditions of the licence is that the animals are retained in approved quarantine premises for up to six months. No exemptions are made for animals that have been vaccinated against rabies. Penalties for smuggling involve imprisonment, unlimited fines and destruction of the animal.

Any animal being imported into the US must have a valid certificate of vaccination against rabies.

For further details apply to the Ministry of Agriculture (Animal Health Division), Hook Rise South, Tolworth, Surbiton, Surrey KT6 7NF.

Souvenirs may be taken out of Yugoslavia without restriction, provided they have been bought with legally imported foreign currency (p. 12), with the exception of items of archaeological, cultural or scientific value, for which permission must be obtained. If in any doubt, check at the time of purchase and keep receipts.

The chart below summarizes what travellers may bring home free of duty. (People under age of 17 are not entitled to tobacco and drinks allowance.)

Duty-free allowances *subject to change*		Bought duty free or outside EEC	Duty and tax paid in EEC
Tobacco	Cigarettes	200	300
	or		
	Cigars *small*	100	150
	or		
	Cigars *large*	50	75
	or		
	Pipe tobacco	250 gm	400 gm
Alcohol	Spirits *over 38.8° proof*	1 litre	1½ litres
	or		
	Fortified or sparkling wine	2 litres	3 litres
	plus		
	Table wine	2 litres	4 litres
Perfume		50 gm	75 gm
Toilet water		250 cc	375 cc
Other goods		£28	£120

Double if you live outside Europe

US customs permit duty-free $300 retail value of purchases per person, 1 quart of liquor per person over 21, and 100 cigars per person.

CURRENCY

The unit of currency is the dinar, divided into 100 paras. Notes are issued in denominations of 10, 20, 50, 100, 500 and 1000 dinars, and coins of 5, 10, 20 and 50 paras, and 1, 2, 5 and 10 dinars.

Travellers' cheques are the safe way of carrying money, but keep a few sterling, dollar or other hard currency notes to meet any unexpected needs at times when exchange offices are closed. You can also use Eurocheques (personal cheques accompanied by a special Eurocheque card available from most banks) which get the same rate of exchange as travellers' cheques in exchange offices displaying the 'ec' (Eurocheque) symbol, though the handling fee will vary. An even more flexible facility is available through the Midland Bank group who will supply a uniform Eurocheque card (small fee) together with Eurocheques which can be used both in the UK and abroad to obtain currency in the usual way or to pay for goods or services in local currency.

Exchange transactions can be made at banks (opening hours p. 25), travel agencies and many hotels, and the rate will not vary. However, Yugoslavia has been taking some severe measures to balance her economic books, so don't change more than you need in case of further devaluation. Unused Yugoslav currency can be re-exchanged when you leave the country as long as you can produce official exchange receipts.

You may bring into Yugoslavia unlimited amounts of foreign currency in cash, travellers' cheques, *etc.* In fact, you will get a better rate if you buy dinars at home, but may only import or export 1500 dinars per person in denominations of 100 dinars or less.

International credit cards are accepted at places displaying appropriate stickers.

Diners, American Express and Carte Blanche are more widely accepted, for example, than Access or Barclaycard.

HOW TO GET THERE

Package Tours A list of tour operators can be obtained from YNTOs abroad (p. 27). In the UK preferably choose a firm that belongs to ABTA (Association of British Travel Agents, 55–57 Newman St., London W1P 4AH), as they will investigate legitimate complaints or recompense you in the unlikely event of the company failing. Package tours have the obvious advantage of taking the hassle out of planning but you are, of course, tied to the arrangements you have paid for. Packages usually work out cheaper unless you do some very thorough homework on the cheapest routes and accommodation. Tour prices drop sharply outside the July–August peak; the best buys, combining good weather and low cost, are in May and early October along the coast. There are also good reductions of 20–50 per cent (according to season) for children, 2–11 years inclusive, sharing a room with a full fare paying adult.

The range of one- or two-centre holidays offers the widest choice. A good combination is a week on the coast with another in the lakes or mountains or touring by coach. Naturist centres (p. 19) feature in a number of arrangements. Though conditions are ideal for many special interest activities, these are only just beginning to feature in packaged arrangements (some addresses on p. 27).

By Air All direct scheduled flights to Yugoslavia from the UK and North America are operated by JAT (*Jugoslovenski Aerotransport*, Yugoslav Airlines) and from Australia by JAT in pool with Qantas. Most are to Belgrade and/or Zagreb, though other towns and cities are served either by direct or connecting flights (list of Yugoslav airports, p. 14). In summer, for example, there are direct flights to Pula, Dubrovnik and Split. JAT and other national airlines link many European cities with Yugoslavia.

The full fare is expensive, but a variety of excursion fares reduces the cost considerably, though they impose certain time restrictions which you will need to check. There are modest airport taxes on international and domestic flights from Yugoslav airports.

It is possible to buy charter-flight-only tickets from the UK to Yugoslavia through Thomson Holidays (Britannia Airways) and some other companies. Check the advertisements in the Sunday papers or weekly *Time Out* magazine, and don't part with any money until you are satisfied with all the conditions.

By Bus There is no Europabus service, though some companies operating to Athens may have stop-offs in Yugoslavia; do make quite sure that such operators have the proper licences. The journey London–Belgrade takes two days (including night travel) and is cheap but tiring. Check advertisements in the weekly *Time Out* magazine.

By Rail This offers no advantage unless you are a railway enthusiast or qualify for the fixed-price Inter-Rail Youth Card for under-26s or Inter-Rail Senior Pass for men over 65 and women over 60, valid in most European countries including Yugoslavia. Otherwise second-class return fares from London to Belgrade cost a little less than the cheapest low season scheduled return air fare. On some routes trains are often packed with Turks as well as Yugoslavs going to and from jobs in western Europe, and refreshment and toilet facilities may be inadequate. The best and most direct route, with sleeping cars and couchettes available, is London – Dover – Ostende – Brussels – Munich – Salzburg – Ljubljana – Zagreb, taking about 30 hours. Other routes involve a change in Paris or Venice. Transalpino (address p. 27) specializes in low-priced rail travel for the under-26s.

By Car The approximate distance by the most direct route from Calais or Oostende via Germany (Cologne–Munich) and Austria to Zagreb is 1450km/900mi; to Belgrade 1850km/1150mi. A longer but more attractive route is through France, Switzerland and northern Italy (Milan–Trieste). Car sleeper services operate during the summer from a number of places in Belgium and Germany to Ljubljana, and from Boulogne, Brussels and Paris to Milan (see also Internal Travel).

Shipping companies with services to the appropriate Channel ports are as follows: Boulogne (Hoverspeed, P & O Ferries, Sealink), Calais (Hoverspeed, Sealink, Townsend Thoresen), Dieppe (Sealink), Dunkerque (Sealink, Sally Viking Line), Oostende (Sealink), Zeebrugge (North Sea Ferries, Townsend Thoresen).

The main crossing points into Yugoslavia from western Europe by road are:
from Italy Trieste–Koper to Istrian coast
Trieste–Kozina to Rijeka
Trieste–Fernetti–Sežana to Postojna and Ljubljana

Udine–Gorizia–Nova Gorica to Julian Alps or Ljubljana
Tarvisio–Predel Pass–Bovec to Julian Alps
Tarvisio–Fusine Laghi–Rateče-Kranjska Gora to Julian Alps
from Austria Villach–Wurzen Pass–Podkoren–Kranjska Gora to Julian Alps or Ljubljana
Klagenfurt–Loibl/Ljubelj Pass–Tržič to Kranj and Ljubljana
Graz–Šentilj–Maribor to Celje and Ljubljana or Varaždin and Zagreb

INTERNAL TRAVEL

There is no digest covering all forms of public transport.

Domestic Air Services These are operated by JAT to the following centres: Belgrade, Dubrovnik, Ljubljana, Maribor, Ohrid, Osijek, Pula, Rijeka, Sarajevo, Skopje, Split, Titograd, Tivat, Zadar, Zagreb. Fares are low, but demand is extremely heavy on some routes, so advance reservation is recommended.

Railways The publication *Red Vožnje* details all rail timetables. It includes an introductory text in English, some ferry and bus services and can be bought in Yugoslavia. The main rail artery, which is also part of the trans-Europe network, links Ljubljana, Zagreb, Belgrade, Niš and Skopje, crossing the entire country from north west to south east. Lateral routes link this with the coast at Koper, Pula, Rijeka, Zadar, Šibenik, Split, Kardeljevo and Bar. There is no rail route along the coast. Train journeys are often scenically splendid if time-consuming, the most spectacular being from Belgrade to Bar (Montenegro), a masterpiece of engineering involving scores of bridges and tunnels. Most trains are diesel driven and restaurant cars, couchettes or sleepers are provided on longer journeys. Cars are carried on many routes, including all those linking main inland cities with the coast. Passenger fares are low (lower than by bus). The Inter-Rail Youth Card and Inter-Rail Senior Pass (see p. 13) are valid in Yugoslavia.

Buses There is a very well-developed network of express buses linking main centres and slower buses serving the villages. You may find it surprising in this socialist country that so many different companies operate in competition with each other on similar routes. They all function on the workers' self-management system (p. 6). The main problem is getting timetables relating to parts of the country other than the one you are in; for these you are entirely in the hands of travel agency or bus station staff whose knowledge and degree of accuracy vary! A seat reservation is strongly recommended, but is only possible if you are embarking at a terminal.

Coastal Traffic There is an intensive network of services, both up and down the coast and from mainland centres to the islands. These range from express routes linking main towns to a bevy of smaller passenger and car ferries and hydrofoils on shorter routes. They are all operated by Jadrolinija (address p. 27) whose timetables are available from YNTOs abroad and from local travel agencies. The express service takes about 24 hours for the full length of the coast from Rijeka to Dubrovnik or Bar; there are cabins and restaurant facilities.

Note that out of the main tourist season, some services are reduced or cancelled. As some are geared to the needs of the islanders, leaving extremely early in the morning and returning in the afternoon, it may be necessary to stay overnight on remoter islands. But dawn over the Adriatic can be magical, and the company of villagers off to market makes a refreshing change from fellow tourists! Main car ferry services are mentioned in the gazetteer, but check locally on the many additional passenger ferries between smaller communities and the mainland.

Main centres such as Rijeka, Zadar, Split, Dubrovnik and Bar are also linked by sea with Italian or Greek ports.

River Traffic A hydrofoil operates in summer from Belgrade down the Danube to Kladovo via the spectacular Iron Gates.

City Transport Yugoslavia has no underground. Most city centres are served by trams or trolleys, the suburbs by buses. You can usually buy your ticket on the vehicle or (in some cases, eg in Belgrade or Sarajevo, at lower cost) from kiosks near stops.

Taxis In towns these are clearly marked (Taksi) and usually show a light when free. There are ranks, but taxis can also be stopped on the street. Fares are metered, but for longer journeys and in country districts it is better to agree the price before starting the journey.

Excursions (See also Entertainment.) Sightseeing tours are arranged in all cities and larger resorts. Many Yugoslav travel agents organize half- or full-day excursions to places of interest, as well as longer tours of several days, some of them focusing on specific themes such as wine tasting or medieval monasteries. Picnics, where fish is cooked over a fire in the open air, and mountain barbecues are also popular.

Car Rental This is widely available through international car rental firms or travel agencies throughout the country, or you can book a fly-drive arrangement from the UK. Charges are about the same as in the UK, but vehicle maintenance is not always what it should be.

IF YOU ARE MOTORING

Driving in Yugoslavia requires vigilance. Many main roads are relatively narrow, frequently sinuous and, especially in summer, often congested. Yugoslav motorists tend to drive fast, manoeuvre unpredictably and rarely seem to use their mirrors. In quieter, more traffic-free areas livestock, non-motorized vehicles and inattentive country folk present a different hazard. That said, though Yugoslavs are not the most disciplined road users, they have a sneaking admiration for the reputed courtesy of the British motorist, and it is far better to encourage this than attempt to set up in competition, whatever the temptation! There are some truly stunning routes and no better way to experience the huge variety of the Yugoslav countryside than through the freedom of your own four wheels. Members of their own national motoring organizations can take advantage of special touring services and benefit also from certain facilities offered by their counterparts in Yugoslavia.

Documents Citizens of any country taking their own car into Yugoslavia will need their national driving licence (not a provisional); car registration certificate; an oval identity sticker (GB or equivalent); and International Green Card of Insurance, obtainable from your insurance company by paying a small extra premium. Check with them that you are adequately covered for your needs, including damage while in transit.

Fuel At the time of going to press, foreign motorists must buy petrol coupons for hard currency. These are on sale at all border points (where you can buy coupons offering a 10 per cent discount on pump prices), or in many Yugoslav towns (list available from YNTOs abroad), or through their national motoring organization, AMSJ. Unused coupons can be cashed in at the border on leaving. Two grades of fuel are available: premium 86 octane, and super 98 octane. Filling stations are plentiful in towns and on main roads, but make sure your tank is topped up if you are wandering off into remoter regions.

Adriatic Highway

Rules of the Road

You drive on the right and, under most circumstances, give way to traffic from the right unless it is clearly marked that you have priority. Trams and buses always have priority and should never be overtaken when they are unloading passengers. The same applies to vehicles carrying children.

Roads and Road Signs There has been a great improvement in the road network in recent years, including short but expanding stretches of motorway. The annually revised tourist map from YNTOs abroad clearly shows the latest situation and indicates stretches on which toll charges apply. However, although main roads are usually good, the nature of the terrain often obliges them to be steep and winding and many – including the far-famed Adriatic Highway – are narrow for the demands made upon them, especially at the height of the season when hordes of motorized tourists join the ever-growing local traffic and fleets of heavy long-distance lorries. There is the additional distraction of the scenery: so, if you want to admire the view, pull off the road and stop. Minor roads are often unsurfaced, but may be better than those which are surfaced but pot-holed. Either way, allow extra time for any journey planned away from main circuits.

Traffic symbols are those used internationally. A road numbering system exists only for international 'E'-classified roads. Signposting is good on main routes but becomes a bit of an adventure if you stray. Signposts show the Latin alphabet in Slovenia and Croatia and mainly Latin or both alphabets in the rest of the country, though you will find exceptions when Cyrillic only is used in remoter areas of the interior.

Lights It is not compulsory but advisable to adapt headlights suited to left-hand traffic with some opaque material. Dipped headlights must be used at all times by motorcyclists and moped riders and by motorists whenever visibility is poor.

Safety Crash helmets must be worn by all

motorcyclists and their passengers. The use of seat belts by driver and front-seat passenger is compulsory; children under the age of twelve or persons under the influence of alcohol should not travel in the front passenger seat. Warning triangles should be carried.

Horns The use of the horn is discouraged, except in an emergency, and horns with changing tones or melodies are forbidden.

Speed Limits The limit in built-up areas is 60kph/37mph; outside built-up areas 80kph/50mph, sometimes varied to 100kph/62mph and 120kph/75mph on motorways. If you are towing a caravan, the maximum is 80kph/50mph. Speeding is the most common offence, and fines are imposed on the spot; the greater the speed the higher the fine!

Parking This is a major problem in the bigger towns. In some cities there are meters (inexpensive) and, in one or two cities, multi-storey garages, as well as free car parking, but never enough. It is a particular problem if you are staying in a city centre hotel without its own garage, and there is no obvious solution. Illegally parked cars may be removed by a machine known as a 'spider', in which case the owner must retrieve his car himself at quite heavy cost.

Breakdown or Accident The Yugoslav Automobile Association (AMSJ, address p. 27) operates an assistance and information service and has specialized vehicles and mechanics stationed at over 120 bases, open 0800–2000. These bases and their yellow vehicles, which patrol main roads, are marked *Pomoć-Informacije*. To summon this service in the case of breakdown, telephone 987 or ask a passing motorist or police patrol to get help for you.

Authorized service stations dealing with most makes of car are to be found only in larger towns and tourist resorts, and it is advisable to carry essential spare parts. Private garages also offer repair and towing services, but you should get an estimate first. Urgent orders for locally unavailable spare parts can be made through the AMSJ if you are a member of your own national motoring organization.

In the case of a traffic accident resulting in major damage or injury, you must remain on the spot, take necessary steps to eliminate any risk of further accident and allow free flow of traffic. If the vehicle is causing a serious obstruction, mark its position before independent witnesses and, if possible, take a photograph of the scene. You are legally obliged to notify the police (telephone 92) and, in case of injury, ambulance (94). Members of their own national motoring organizations can, if necessary, obtain legal advice through lawyers associated with AMSJ.

You are also legally obliged to stop and offer assistance if you come across an accident in which you are not involved.

Alcohol A driver suspected of being under the influence of alcohol must submit to a breath test or medical examination. An alcohol content in the blood above 50mg/ml is an offence punishable by a fine, imprisonment and/or suspension of driving licence. If you drink, *don't* drive.

Car-carrying Trains See p. 14.

WHERE TO STAY

There are no central booking offices specifically for accommodation in Yugoslav towns; if you have any problems, go to the local tourist office or a travel agency (Information, p. 25) who can advise on, and usually book, all forms of accommodation.

Hotels All hotels are classified according to federal law and inspected by local authorities. They are run on the workers' self-management system (p. 6), either individually or as part of a group enterprise. Most are listed in a free booklet revised annually and available from YNTOs abroad. This indicates for each hotel the category (de luxe, A, B, C or D), the number of beds, prices of rooms with and without bath or shower, per night or with half or full board. Though the classification system is a helpful indication of standard, it is not infallible. Some recently built Bs are almost indistinguishable from As, and a modern C can be better than an aging B. Service also varies greatly, whether in popular resorts where staff are often overworked in high season, or in less frequented regions, especially in the interior, where the amenities of glossy new premises may not yet be matched by staff know-how. Plumbing can be unpredictable and water supplies intermittent in some areas. Broadly speaking, the further north and west you are, the more reliable most things are.

Note that many modern hotel complexes are built at some distance from the centre under which they are listed. Some of them are quite self-contained and very well equipped with all kinds of recreational and entertainment facilities. These very advantages, however, tend to insulate visitors from the local community and the Yugoslav way of life.

If you value quietness, make sure your room is not overlooking a busy thoroughfare, restaurant terrace or above a disco.

Hotel rates are quoted in US dollars or German Deutschmark (though you pay in dinars). In most towns and cities rates stay the same all year round, but in resorts they vary enormously according to season; in the low season they may be little more than half the high season rate. Full- or half-board rates in the official lists are usually quoted for a minimum stay of three days. A small additional tourist tax varies according to locality and season.

Motels Officially classified I, II and III, a growing number are appearing on the outskirts of towns or along main roads.

Guesthouses These are usually privately run and are most numerous in Slovenia (look for the sign *gostilna*) and Croatia (*gostionica*). They can be charming as well as inexpensive and offer a more intimate contact with the Yugoslav way of life.

Private Accommodation This facility is well developed throughout the country but especially along the coast, and gives an excellent opportunity for closer contact with Yugoslav family life. A special booklet is published annually by the YNTO, giving booking addresses (usually local tourist offices and travel agencies) and prices. Where full- or half-board rates are quoted, meals are taken in a nearby restaurant.

Farmhouses For the moment this type of accommodation is limited to Slovenia, where you can obtain a booklet from Kompas Travel Agency (address on p. 27) giving details of each farm, its accommodation, recreational amenities and even its livestock. Some offer half or full board, and most are in delightfully secluded mountain settings.

Self Catering This is a relatively new but rapidly expanding facility, especially in or near popular coastal centres. Accommodation is usually in apartments in a purpose-built complex with supermarket, restaurants and recreational amenities.

Camping An annually revised list of campsites, giving details of category, amenities and prices, is available from YNTOs. Sites in popular holiday areas get extremely crowded in summer, so start looking early. Small chalets may be rented on some sites. Permission to camp other than at official sites must be obtained from local tourist offices or local authorities – not always very practical in the kind of areas where you are most likely to want an unofficial site! Away from resort areas, considerate campers are unlikely to be bothered, but are nevertheless breaking the law and cannot complain if they find themselves at odds with officialdom.

Youth Accommodation There is a number of well-equipped international youth centres, notably at Bečići (near Budva), Dubrovnik and Rovinj, run by Naromtravel who specialize in youth travel (address p. 27). There is no official list of youth hostels, but student accommodation is available in most towns. The local tourist office can give addresses.

FOOD AND DRINK

National or regional dishes feature in the many folklore evenings held throughout the holiday season, and many hotels include one or two dishes in their menus. Service tends to be somewhat brisk in the big hotels at holiday time. It is well worth trying out some of the smaller restaurants (many of them privately owned) which have burgeoned in recent years. The word for restaurant is *restoran* (РЕСТОРАН), and a fish restaurant *riblji restoran*. A small establishment serving drinks is often called *bife* (БИФЕ).

Some dishes and drinks can be regarded as national, even ubiquitous, but there are also plenty of regional dishes reflecting culinary influences from Yugoslavia's chequered history. In most towns and main resorts you will find restaurants specializing in the food of another region. If it's called *Dalmacija* or after one of the islands, it will almost certainly serve fish; *Lovački rog* invariably offers game; *Bosna* or *Drina* indicates Bosnian specialities.

The most frequently encountered dish of all is *čevapčiči* (small spiced grilled minced beef or mutton rolls), usually served with raw onions and bread. They're very tasty and in many places there are kiosks or small take-away places selling nothing but these. Almost as common are *ražnjiči* (grilled pieces of pork or veal on skewers). Another variation is *pleskavica*, grilled minced beef and mutton with raw onions and red peppers, flattened in the form of a steak.

As elsewhere in the Balkans, minced meat, rice and spices are used as a stuffing for leaves or vegetables such as vine leaves, fresh or pickled cabbage leaves and peppers; the most common dish is *sarma*, using cabbage leaves. *Moussaka*, of course, is another favourite Balkan dish: baked aubergines with minced meat.

In the north, regional food bears the distinct hallmark of a Habsburg past. A Slovenian example is *kmečka pojedina* composed of various sausages, pork, cabbage, potatoes and dumplings. The Slovenes also go in for a variety of interesting sausages (usually pork), such as *pečinica* and *kranjska klobasa*. In Serbian Vojvodina, the Hungarian influence is unmistakable. If you get the opportunity, don't miss *paprikaš*, an incredibly rich soup whose main ingredient may be chicken or fish, simmered infinitely slowly over an open fire (preferably outdoors) with onions and hot peppers, and served with home-made pasta. A better known Serbian dish is *djuveć*, a blending of aubergines and other vegetables, rice and pieces of pork, chicken or mutton, roasted with grated cheese. In Bosnia *Bosanski lonac* (hotpot) also puts the emphasis on a variety of vegetables, especially cabbage, cooked for several hours with beef or mutton in a special earthenware pot. It is in Bosnia-Herzegovina, though also elsewhere, that you will find innumerable eating places known as *ašcinica* serving local specialities such as *burek* in which layers of light pastry alternate with various tasty fillings such as meat, cheese, potato, spinach or pumpkin. They make an excellent quick snack. Many such dishes are eaten with *kiselo mljeko*, a kind of yoghourt. *Kajmak*, a salty cream cheese, is also used a lot in cooking or as an accompaniment.

Pršut, smoked ham (though it may be air-dried in some areas), is at its best when cut almost transparently thin, and is frequently served as an appetizer. You'll probably also get it as part of *marenda*, a kind of mid-morning brunch popular along the coast. It often comes with a selection of pickled gherkins, sweet peppers, tomatoes, onions, and so on. These, along with cucumber and sometimes a topping of grated cheese, are the ingredients for a variety of salads which are offered with nearly every meal. Another interesting mixture is *ajvar*: baked aubergines seasoned with onions, garlic and chilli.

The Yugoslavs are great meat-eaters, and the quality is usually good, but there is also plenty of fish which is reflected in the large number of fish restaurants. In the mountains you can expect excellent grilled trout, and major waterways such as the Danube contribute a selection ranging from pike, perch and carp to catfish and various members of the sturgeon family, such as sterlet. Along the coast, *brodet* is a

rich fish soup incorporating potatoes and vegetables, but fish such as plaice, mackerel, red or grey mullet, squid, are mostly charcoal grilled. Excellent oysters are produced in one or two coastal areas. Lobster, crab, mussels are commonly on offer at seafood restaurants, as well as less easily translatable fare like the finger-length *prstaci*, which live inside stones.

Desserts are invariably rich and sweet. In the centre and south, *kadaif* (pastry with butter, sugar and raisins), *tufahija* (apple stuffed with nuts) and *baklava* (thin pastry with a filling of syrup and nuts) are clearly among the remnants of the Turkish heritage. Central European influences are equally noticeable further north in the creamy cakes, the pastry-and-fruit *strudla*, fruit dumplings, and *palačinke* (pancakes) which are particularly good when served *sa šatoom*: a mixture of egg, nuts, sugar and wine.

The national beverage is Turkish coffee (*turska kava* or simply *turska*), thick, strong and usually sweet (ask for *bez šećera* if you want it without sugar). It's served in small cups which become smaller and without handles as you travel south and inland. In the tourist resorts, quite a few places now serve only *espresso* or a fairly revolting instant coffee usually known as *Nes*, and this is a pity for a really good *turska* is hard to beat. Breakfast coffee, as we know it, is usually pretty awful. Tea is normally just a bag in a glass of hot water, but there are some good herbal teas about.

Yugoslav beer (*pivo*) is rather light. Most visitors are more interested in the many wines (*vino*), some of which are excellent. Broadly speaking, those from inland regions (*Ljutomer Riesling, Sylvaner* and *Traminer* from Slovenia and *Žilavka* from the Mostar region of Herzegovina) are light, while those of the coastal areas are more full bodied, mostly red and, with a few exceptions, dry. One of the best Dalmatian wines is *Dingač* which should come from a very limited part of the Pelješac peninsula, though this is not always the case. *Plavac* is another good Dalmatian product. From the island of

Restaurant in the old Sveta Klara convent, Dubrovnik

Korčula comes the extremely heady, amber-coloured *Grk*, and the lighter (in all senses) *Blato*. Be wary also of the potent *Teran*, a dark red Istrian wine. Other wines to try are *Postup* (white) from Pelješac, *Vranac* (red) and *Krstač* (white) from Montenegro, and *Kratošija* (red) from Macedonia.

The Yugoslavs quite often add soda to white wine and call it *špricer*, which is refreshing as well as less alcoholic. If you want to avoid alcohol, though, there are any number of good Yugoslav mineral waters and some delicious fruit juices (*voćni sok*) in which you can really taste the fruit.

The national strong drink is *šljivovica* (plum brandy), and there are many brands, ranging from the very rough to the excellent; *Prepečenica* and *Badel* are good ones to look out for. *Rakija* is the general name for a group of strong spirits, though if you are offered one it will often turn out to be *šljivovica*. There is also a host of strong drinks made from fruits or herbs, such as *pelinkovac* (very bitter, flavoured with wormwood), *travarica* (marjoram and mint), *lozovača* (grapes) and, of course, *maraschino*, a very sweet liqueur made from maraschino cherries.

ENJOY YOURSELF

The varied terrain of Yugoslavia makes it ideal for many outdoor activities, and amenities for the more popular pursuits exist at many resorts. As yet, however, there is no coordinated organization to help the more serious devotees of activities such as climbing, kayaking, angling, bird watching, which are likely to require local expertise of a particular kind. As sources of information are not centralized, your best hope is to contact the Tourist Association for the republic concerned. They or YNTOs abroad can give you addresses of the associations appropriate to your interest. Or you can get in touch with the relevant local club on the spot. A shared enthusiasm will usually overcome almost any obstacle. A few Yugoslav travel agencies and one or two UK tour operators specialize in particular activities. (See Useful Addresses.)

Water Sports

It is worth bearing in mind some characteristic **winds** which can blow up with great suddenness and vigour along the coast. *Bura* is a cold, gusty, dry wind that blows from NNE or ENE mainly in winter, but sometimes briefly in summer. *Yugo*, a warm humid wind from ESE and SSE, creating considerable waves and

bringing rain, can blow at any time, but mainly in winter. The steady *maestral* is the most frequent, occurring between 1000 and 1800, from SSW to WNW; also known by various local names. Storms are most frequent between June and September, chiefly in July and August, but are of short duration and more likely in the north Adriatic (where they mostly occur at night).

Swimming There is wonderful bathing off this heavily indented coast and its islands. The currents that weave through the archipelagoes keep the waters gloriously clear – the only exception being very near small pockets of industry around Rijeka, Split and Bar. The Yugoslav authorities are not complacent about pollution and have taken an active part in a number of international programmes concerned with conditions in the Mediterranean and its offshoots. There are no tides to worry about but note the comment above concerning characteristic winds.

Most of the bathing is off rocks, shingle or stone beaches, or quite attractive man-made bathing areas of paving stones set among the rocks. When the Yugoslavs describe a beach as sandy, they often simply mean that you have sand underfoot once you enter the water. The only extensive stretch of truly fine sands is at Ulcinj (p. 85), though there are beaches of coarse sand, small stones or pebbles in many other places. In principle, all beaches are public, but in practice some smaller ones are only accessible from the hotels built beside them.

Naturist Bathing The Yugoslav coast, extremely popular with naturists, offers a number of special fully-equipped centres. In addition there are beaches reserved for naturist bathing within easy reach of over a score of resorts including Bol, Cavtat, Dubrovnik, Hvar, Korčula, Orebić, Poreč, Primošten, Rovinj, Tučepi, Ulcinj, Umag and Zadar. UK tour operators featuring naturist packages are on p. 27.

Fishing and Angling Sea angling (with rod) does not require a permit and fishing trips, with rods provided, are arranged from many coastal resorts. You will need a permit for fishing in rivers and lakes and this is issued by angling clubs, municipal authorities and, in some places, by hotels or tourist offices.

Other forms of sea fishing (including underwater) may only be done with certain equipment (excluding diving gear) and are restricted in certain areas so you must check the fairly complex local regulations on the spot. Permits are issued by municipal authorities, or you can join one of the Yugoslav sea fishing, underwater fishing or diving societies.

Diving It is forbidden to go underwater fishing with diving gear; a police permit is required for the use of diving gear and underwater photography. Compressed air can be obtained in main coastal centres.

Sailing Visiting yachts must register at the nearest port open to international traffic (which means all coastal towns and many resorts) and obtain a sailing permit from the port authorities. They should carry valid sailing documents appropriate to their own country and certificates of seamanship for all members of the crew.

These are idyllic sailing waters and there is no more satisfying way of exploring this very beautiful coast for the suitably experienced. Strong winds can blow up very rapidly, however, (see p. 19) and even though lee shelter is usually of easy access, proper caution is common sense, especially with regard to secure mooring at night. Flotilla sailing holidays, suitable for both novices and the experienced, are marketed by some UK tour operators and, if you've ever had the urge to hoist a mainsail, must provide the perfect holiday.

Water Skiing Available at many resorts.

Wind Surfing Available at an increasing number of resorts.

Canoeing, Kayaking, Rafting Despite the proliferation of hydro-electric installations there are still plenty of splendid waters for the experienced, though rental of equipment is limited. Canoeists and kayakists would do best to contact clubs, the best rivers being in Slovenia, Croatia and Bosnia-Herzegovina. Some exciting rafting trips are arranged, with prior notice, on the rivers Drina in Bosnia-Herzegovina (contact Unisturist) and Tara in Montenegro (contact Montenegroturist). These organizations put you in the hands of experts; on longer trips overnights are spent in camp with equipment provided.

Sports & Activities

Field Studies Varied terrain, from the Danubian plains to such heights as the Julian Alps of Slovenia and Durmitor of Montenegro, yields a rich variety of habitat for birds and flowers. Local experts are limited in number, but delighted to meet visiting soul mates – try the local tourist office.

Golf The good (and only) 18-hole course is at Bled, Slovenia.

Hunting Facilities are well organized, with transport laid on to the usually remote hunting grounds. Accommodation is provided in hunting lodges or hotels, and guides are available; but, as ever, it is an expensive sport. Yugoslav travel agencies specializing in hunting trips are Emona Globtour, Generalturist and Unisturist; Generalturist in particular have a big department dealing only with this activity and have their own hunting grounds. You can also contact the Hunting Association (*Lovački drustvo*) which is in all the appropriate localities. Hunting seasons vary according to game and region, but are mainly in the autumn and winter.

Riding The most notable centre is the famous Lippizaner stud farm at Lipica, Slovenia (p. 35). Riding can be arranged here by the hour, the day or the week, with instruction. Tours are also arranged from the UK.

Village Tourism This fairly recent addition to the tourist scene is an attempt to provide opportunities for visitors to enjoy closer contact with rural Yugoslavia. It can mean anything from visits to local craftsmen, attendance at some traditional event, a barbecue with mountain shepherds or picnic in a fishing community.

Walking and Climbing Excellent networks of marked trails are established through many mountain regions, and overnight accommodation is available in mountain hostels or refuges. Local tourist offices or the Tourist Association for each republic (addresses, p. 27) can provide general information and put you in touch with the appropriate mountaineering association (*Planinarski savez*). Local climbing clubs welcome visitors. Recommended areas are the Julian Alps of Slovenia, the mountain ranges around Sarajevo in Bosnia-Herzegovina, Durmitor mountain in Montenegro, and Šar-Planina in Macedonia, but there are plenty of others. The E6 hiking trail crosses Slovenia from west of Maribor to near Rijeka and is 250km/155mi in length. Some walking holidays are arranged from the UK.

Winter Sports A number of Yugoslav resorts now offer skiing conditions and amenities comparable to those of many better known areas and at reasonable cost. The best are to be found in the mountains of Slovenia (especially Kranjska Gora and Bovec), and near Sarajevo (site of the 1984 Winter Olympics) in Bosnia-Herzegovina. Kopaonik in Serbia and Šar-Planina in Macedonia are rapidly developing and interesting alternatives if you want to escape from your compatriots. Winter sports packages can be arranged from the UK.

ENTERTAINMENT

The main regular annual events are listed on p. 22, and precise dates are given in the annually revised calendar of events available from YNTOs. One entertaining daily event that will not be listed, however, is the *korzo*. This is the early evening stroll engaged in by most of the community: a sociable amble up one side and back down the other of a central street or square (often made traffic-free for that purpose) or along the waterfront of a coastal community. Its presence is usually heralded from quite a distance by a low hum, as of a swarm of bees, growing into a tremendous babble as you turn the final corner and are caught up in this convivial throng. It is an occasion for greetings and gossip, for seeing and being seen, and many a courtship has begun just here. The *korzo* usually begins as dusk falls and ends, as if at an unseen signal, around 2030. Within minutes the streets are virtually deserted, though many of the participants will reappear later to crowd the cafés, bars and restaurants.

Folklore (See also The Arts.) Though the 'real thing' has often given way, as in so many countries, to canned entertainment, folklore remains a living tradition in remoter areas and is kept very much alive elsewhere. Most young Yugoslavs nowadays are a generation or more removed from the rural way of life and the self-entertainment of their elders, but many of them are genuinely attracted to their folk heritage. Nearly every locality has its folklore group, often performing to a very high standard. The better known ones, such as *Kolo* or *Branko Krsmanović* of Belgrade, *Lada* of Zagreb, *Tanec* of Skopje, *Lindjo* of Dubrovnik, are worth going out of your way to see; but small local groups in resort hotels and restaurants often perform with artistry, vigour and every appearance of enjoying themselves.

More specific traditional events have become tourist attractions in their own right. The peasant weddings of Plitvice, Bled and remote Galičnik now also draw foreign couples who come to plight their troth. Other events originated in more or less historic occasions. The best known is Korčula's *Moreška* Sword Dance which has toured widely abroad. This spectacular and exhausting dance dates back to the 16th century and depicts the eternal struggle against oppression, here represented by a girl (possibly symbolizing Korčula) seized by foreign conquerors. It is performed amid clashing swords by two groups of seven dancers dressed in red and black costumes sewn with golden thread. All the dancers are local amateurs whose dedication to long hours of rehearsal results in a very polished performance. The *Alka* of Sinj commemorates the victory over the Turkish army in 1715. This

equestrian tilting-at-the-ring contest displays not only skilled horsemanship but also the picturesque uniforms and weapons of the period. Countless minor events take place around the country and may be all the more fun for being unexpected. Enquire at the local tourist office. If you are interested in a more comprehensive view of regional costume and dance styles, try and get to one of the larger folklore festivals, such as those at Zagreb and Ohrid.

Festivals Almost every town and resort has some form of summer festivity, many made memorable by the historic setting. Topping the list undoubtedly is the Dubrovnik Summer Festival whose quality and backdrop probably compensate for the crowds and summer heat which accompany it. The programme of drama, ballet, music and folklore, includes many guest artists of international standing, and over 100 performances take place against the magnificent settings of historic buildings in the city. The sound of *Hamlet* in Serbo-Croat may seem strange, but to see the play unfold against the craggy walls of Fort Lovrjenac is unforgettable. Advance programmes are available from YNTOs abroad, though usually regrettably late.

Most of the other summer festivals last a month or two, and among their attractions are settings such as the Križanke complex in Ljubljana, the old Bohemian quarter of Skadarlija in Belgrade, Diocletian's Palace at Split, the ancient churches of Zadar and Šibenik, the old streets and squares of Zagreb's Upper Town. Programmes usually combine most forms of the dramatic arts, though the focus may be more specific, *eg* the Yugoslav Film Festival in the stunning setting of Pula's Roman amphitheatre, the Festival of Children in Sibenik, or Poetry Evenings in Struga.

One essentially Yugoslav occasion, when the emphasis is on sporting and folklore events, is the nationwide celebration culminating in *Dan Mladosti* (Youth Day) in Belgrade. This commemorates the late President Tito's birthday and is preceded by several weeks of programmes throughout the country. During this time a specially carved *štafeta* (baton) is carried by relay-runners along a predetermined route, its passage through each locality accompanied by speeches, parades and other happenings. Labour Day celebrations have their share of parades, too, but this is also very much a day for family outings, open-air concerts and folklore and sporting events.

Theatre and Cinema (See also Festivals above.) The dramatic theatre poses obvious language problems, but there is very good opera in Belgrade and Zagreb, with Ljubljana and Sarajevo not far behind. Puppet theatres are popular and of a rather high standard. Foreign films are shown in their original language.

Night Life There are night clubs and a casino or two in the cities and a few of the bigger resorts, and discos multiply annually. The most usual evening entertainment is provided by folk and pop groups – often playing far too loudly, which does not seem to prevent the Yugoslavs from indulging in two of their favourite pastimes: discussion and argument! Away from the tourist circuit, in central and southern inland areas, it is not usual even today to see unaccompanied women in bars and restaurants other than tourist establishments. Foreign women who decide to challenge this long-standing tradition are, however, unlikely to suffer more than a few stares.

Moreška Sword Dance, Korčula

FESTIVALS & EVENTS

Check precise dates or any changes with the latest calendar from YNTOs

March–June	Belgrade, Zagreb, Ljubljana and other major cities	Concert and theatre season, including opera, ballet, folklore, with national and international guest performances.
late April	Zagreb	International Spring Fair: major trade exhibition of consumer goods.
1–2 May	Nationwide	Labour Day celebrations, with parades, sporting and cultural events.
2nd week May	Belgrade	Festival of pop music.
25 May	Belgrade	Youth Day: culmination of the programme in honour of Tito's birthday (p. 21).

weekend in late May	Plitvice	Plitvice Wedding: folklore event with multiple wedding of couples from various countries.
late May–early June	Novi Sad	Yugoslav Theatre Festival.
May–Sept.	Korčula	*Moreška* Sword Dance, every Thurs.; highly dramatic event dating from 16th century (p. 21).
May–Dec.	Belgrade	Skadarlija Evenings: street entertainment in old Bohemian quarter of the city.
June	Rijeka, Pula and other coastal centres of Istria and Kvarner	Melodies of Istria and Quarnero: traditional festival of songs of the region.
mid June–end Aug.	Bled	Folklore evenings every Wed.; classical concerts every Mon.
mid June	Ljubljana	International Jazz Festival.
late June	Šibenik	Yugoslav Festival of Children with international participation.
late June	Ljubljana	Ohcet v Ljubljani: folklore celebration with traditional wedding of couples from several countries.
late June–late Aug.	Ljubljana	International Summer Festival: cultural events. Coincides with Yugoslav opera or ballet festival in alternate years.
late June–late Sept.	Herceg-novi	Open-air drama and musical performances.
early July	Split	Melodies of the Adriatic: festival of light music with sea as main theme.
early July	Niš	Yugoslav choral festival.
10 July–25 Aug.	Dubrovnik	Dubrovnik Summer Festival: outstanding international cultural event of music, drama, ballet, folklore, against historic settings in this mellow old city (p. 21).
12 July–20 Aug.	Ohrid	Ohrid Summer Festival: cultural and folklore events including classical concerts in St Sofia Church. During July, the colourful Balkan Festival of Original Folk Dances and Songs is held in the fortress.
2nd weekend July	Galičnik	Galičnik Wedding: folklore event of special note, featuring old wedding customs.
weekend mid July	Bohinj	Peasant Wedding: folklore event.

mid July–mid Aug.	Split	Split Summer Festival: opera, ballet, drama, folklore, music of all kinds.
mid July–end Aug.	Šibenik	Šibenik Summer: concerts and folklore in the open air and Cathedral.
late July	Zagreb	International Review of Original Folklore: outstanding event with some 80 groups from five continents performing in the city streets and squares.
late July–early Aug.	Pula	Festival of Yugoslav feature films held in Roman amphitheatre.
July–Aug.	Zadar	Musical evenings in historic church of St Donat.
July–Sept.	Opatija	Opatija Summer Festival: cultural and other events including open-air concerts and folklore performances.
July–mid Sept.	Belgrade	Belgrade Summer: review of experimental and traditional theatre, music, films.
July–mid Sept.	Zagreb	Zagreb Summer: open-air cultural events.
1 Aug.	Sinj	*Alka* (tilting-at-the-ring) traditional equestrian event (p. 21).
weekend early Aug.	Bled	Traditional peasant weddings.
late Aug.	Ohrid	Festival of Old Town Songs: traditional Macedonian songs and costumes.
end Aug.–early Sept.	Ljubljana	International Fair of Wine and other beverages.
end Aug.	Struga	Struga Evenings of Poetry with international participation.
3–5 Sept.	Požarevac	International Ljubičevo Equestrian Games: equestrian events and stunts.
mid Sept.	Maribor	Joyous Autumn: event with rural and travel theme.
mid Sept.	Zagreb	International Autumn Fair: major exhibition of science and technology.
2nd half Sept.	Belgrade	BITEF (Belgrade International Theatre Festival): outstanding event focusing on the modern theatre.
3–7 Oct.	Belgrade	Joy of Europe: festival of European children's folk songs and dances.
7–19 Oct.	Belgrade	BEMUS: Belgrade festival of serious music with international participation.

Oct.–Dec.	Belgrade, Zagreb, Ljubljana and other major cities	Concert and theatre season (see March–June above).
mid Nov.	Skopje	Festival of popular music.
end Dec.	Hvar	New Year sailing regatta.
end Dec.	Mali Lošinj	International underwater fishing contest.

WHAT YOU NEED TO KNOW

Chemist Dispensing chemists are called *Apoteka* (АПОТЕКА). For normal opening hours see Opening Times below, but all main towns will have at least one offering a 24-hour service.

Electricity The standard supply is 220 volts AC but all sockets are of the two-pin continental variety so take an adaptor with you.

Emergencies Emergency telephone numbers, nationwide, are: police – 92, ambulance – 94, breakdown – 987.

Information There is a great deal of useful free literature available from YNTOs abroad. Be as specific as possible about the information you want. Good basics are the annually revised tourist map, hotel rates, lists of campsites and private accommodation, summary of tour operators and their packages, and the latest 'Travel Information' booklet. For guidance on special interests, see the comments on p. 19. Within Yugoslavia, every town and resort has its local tourist office (called *turist biro*, and often marked with the international 'i' sign). The standard varies from well-staffed offices handling private accommodation and undertaking travel reservations, excursion bookings, *etc*, to small kiosks equipped only with a handful of hotel brochures. In addition, there is usually one travel agency or more (in major towns, many) geared to handle all the normal tourist services. A few agencies specialize in certain fields such as fishing, hunting, cultural tours, and so on.

It can often be difficult to get accurate information about areas other than the one you are in. However, each of the six republics has one or two main travel agencies which are likely to be the best informed for that part of the country, and each has many branch offices in the other republics. The principal agencies are given under Useful Addresses. Broadly speaking, the further south or east you go, the more patiently you will need to persevere in your quest for hard facts!

Museums and Monuments Opening hours for major museums are normally 0900 or 1000–1200 or 1300, and some or most afternoons from 1600 or 1700–1800 or 1900. The usual day of closure is Monday, but may be Tuesday. For smaller museums and other monuments, the hours vary widely and it is essential to check locally. This is particularly important in the case of the beautiful but often remote churches and monasteries of Serbia, Macedonia and Montenegro, some of which entail a substantial mileage. Entrance fees are low and though explanatory texts are rarely in English, it is quite often possible to buy descriptive booklets in several foreign languages at very reasonable cost.

Newspapers and Foreign News In principle, foreign newspapers and magazines are on sale at some kiosks and main hotels in all major cities and main resorts, though availability varies with the state of the economy. A number of local radio stations, notably those of Zagreb and Ljubljana, broadcast news and information bulletins in English most days.

Opening Times (See also Museums above.) These vary considerably. In cities, many shops are open non-stop from 0800–2000 (Saturdays 0800–1500), while others follow the popular practice of a long lunch break and open 0800–1200 and 1700–2000. Food shops start much earlier, often operating from 0530 or 0600–0930 and 1600–1900, and sometimes Sunday mornings. Markets are open in the mornings from 0530. Banking hours are 0700–1900 (Saturdays 0700–1300), but may vary according to place.

Photography Places where photography is prohibited are usually (but not infallibly) clearly marked and restrictions must be strictly observed. Misunderstandings have arisen between officialdom and over-zealous photographers, so if in doubt, check first. Frontiers and military zones are obviously sensitive areas.

Police They are called *milicija* (МИЛИЦИА) and wear a blue-grey uniform. They are usually friendly and helpful.

Post Post office buildings are marked *Pošta* (ПОШТА). Main offices are open 0700–1900 Monday-Saturday, more limited hours on Sunday. Post boxes are painted red or yellow. Stamps can also be bought at some newspaper kiosks selling postcards.

Public Holidays National holidays are 1 and 2 Jan., 1 and 2 May, 4 July (Partisan Day), 29 and 30 Nov. (Republic Day). Republican national days are 7 July (Serbia), 13 July (Montenegro), 22 July (Slovenia), 27 July (Croatia and Bosnia-Herzegovina), 2 August and 11 October (Macedonia).

Shopping (See also Opening Times above). Yugoslavia's wealth of artisan skills and varied cultural influences have resulted in a rich legacy of arts and crafts ranging from articles of practical everyday use to purely decorative objects. Each republic and, within it, each region and often even each small locality, has its speciality which may be pottery, intricately carved woodwork, filigree jewellery, hand-woven textiles or embroidered blouses, gold, silver or copperware, leather craft or oriental-style carpets of all sizes. Standards vary, of course, but in most regions there is a central enterprise acting as wholesaler for handicrafts produced either in the home or in small factories. Some of these organizations have their own retail outlets where prices may be a little higher but good standards assured. Nowadays there is also a large number of small, privately-owned shops, many specializing in the products of a particular craft practised on the premises. All towns and many villages have markets selling not only fresh produce, but a wide range of handicrafts, and it is worth noting that prices in main city markets are often lower than those in popular tourist resorts. As you travel towards the centre and south of the country, some markets acquire the atmosphere of a bazaar (the one in Sarajevo is especially well known), in which separate sections and even whole streets are dedicated to a particular craft such as leather, copper, silver. You can try a little gentle bargaining here.

In addition to traditional crafts, there are the creations of contemporary painters, sculptors and designers, and plenty of boutiques and galleries in main towns and resorts to sell their work. Yugoslav artists have quite a flair and, though such items are hardly cheap, they are likely to compare favourably with their counterparts in western Europe. If they are of special value, however, they may require an export permit (see Customs, pp. 11–12).

If you are catering for yourself, you will find the best fresh produce on the open-air market stalls. Supermarkets and general food shops are quite well stocked with tinned, packaged and bottled foods of good standard and at reasonable prices. But some areas are subject to unpredictable shortages of quite ordinary items, and a tightening up of the economy has resulted in a spasmodic scarcity of imported goods such as coffee.

Telephones Telephone calls may be made at post offices or from street kiosks. You insert the necessary coins after lifting the receiver. If you cannot get the connection, the money is refunded when you replace the receiver. The newer telephone booths take a wider range of coins for long distance calls. Much of Yugoslavia is now on the automatic dialling system. In some southerly or mountainous regions it is still necessary to go through the operator, which can take time.

Time Yugoslav time is one hour ahead of Greenwich Mean Time (1200 in London is 1300 in Belgrade) all year round. It is therefore on the same time as the UK in summer, but there is one hour's difference in winter.

Tipping Service is not included in restaurant bills, other than in hotels, so add up to 10 per cent depending on the total and the standard of attention received. The same applies to taxis and hairdressers. There is a fixed rate for cloakroom attendants, but you can add a little. Railway porters operate on fixed charges, but expect a tip. Generally Yugoslavs are not at all grabbing by nature, so if anyone is outstandingly helpful, you must simply follow your instincts. Often a small gift will be more appreciated than money, even if it means sending it from home.

Toilets Other than in hotels, restaurants, department stores, museums, railway and bus stations, public toilets are scarce. They range from good to adequate, but flushing systems are often unreliable. Standards are best in the north and along the coast. Have some tissues with you. Symbols for men or women are often used to distinguish between the sexes; otherwise the sign for women is *ženski* (ЖЕНСКИ, and the sign for men is *muški* (МУШКИ).

USEFUL ADDRESSES

(Tel. nos in brackets)
The central tourist body in Yugoslavia is *Turistički savez Jugoslavije*, represented by Yugoslav National Tourist Offices (YNTOs) abroad. Each republic also maintains its own tourist organization (*Turistički savez*) and there are numerous local associations (see Information, p. 25).

Yugoslav National Tourist Offices (abroad): **UK** YNTO, 143 Regent St., London W1R 8AE (01 734 5243). **USA** Rockefeller Center, Suite 210, 630 Fifth Ave, New York, N.Y. 10020 (212 757 2801).

National and Republic Tourist Associations (in Yugoslavia): **Yugoslavia** Turistički savez Jugoslavije, Moše Pijade 8/IV, Belgrade (011 339780). **Bosnia-Herzegovina**, Titova 80/I, Sarajevo (071 22034). **Croatia**, Amruševa 8, Zagreb (041 275528). **Macedonia**, Maršala Tita 39, Skopje (091 231348). **Montenegro**, Bulevar Lenjina 2/I, Titograd (081 41591). **Serbia**, Dobrinjska 11, Belgrade (011 645666). **Slovenia**, Miklošičeva cesta 38/VI, Ljubljana (061 320641).

Consulates (in Yugoslavia): **Canada** Proleterskih brigada 69, Belgrade (011 434524). **UK** Generala Ždanova 46, Belgrade (011 645055); Ilica 12, Zagreb (041 445522); Titova obala 10, Split (058 41464). **USA** Kneza Miloša 50, Belgrade (011 645655); Braće Kavurića 2, Zagreb (041 444800).

Automobile Associations (*Auto-moto savez*): of **Yugoslavia (AMSJ)** Ruzveltova 18, Belgrade (011 419535); of **Bosnia-Herzegovina** Boriše Kovačevića 18, Sarajevo (071 517713); of **Croatia** Draškovićeva 25, Zagreb (041 522522); of **Macedonia** Ivo Ribar Lola 55, Skopje (091 226825); of **Montenegro** Novaka Miloševa 12/II, Titograd (081 43555); of **Serbia** Ivana Milutinovića 58, Belgrade (011 456456); of **Slovenia** Titova cesta 138, Ljubljana (061 342378).

Some major Yugoslav travel agencies (head offices): Atlas, Pile 1, Dubrovnik (050 27333); Centroturist, Bulevar Revolucije 70, Belgrade (011 451142); Dalmacijaturist, Titova Obala 5, Split (058 44666); Emona Globtour, Šmartinska 130, Ljubljana (061 444177); Generalturist, Praška 5, Zagreb (041 446222); Kompas, Pražakova 4, Ljubljana (061 327661); Kvarner Express, Maršala Tita 186, Opatija (051 711111); Montenegroturist, Budva (086-41116); Naromtravel, Moše Pijade 12, Belgrade (011 339030); Palasturist, Gradski trgovski centar, p.p. 52 Skopje (091 238855); Putnik, Dragoslava Jovanovića 1, Belgrade (011 332591); Unisturist, Morića han, Sarači 77, Sarajevo (071 534200).

Some specialist UK tour operators Holiday Fellowship, 142–144 Great North Way, London NW4 1EG (01 203 3381) (walking). Pan Adriatic, 11 Lower John St., London W1R 3PE (01 439 1916) (various special interests by arrangement). Peng Travel, 86 Station Rd, Gidea Park, Essex RM2 6DB (Hornchurch 71832) (naturist). Phoenix Holidays, 29 Thurloe Place, London SW7 2HP (01 581 4674) (naturist, flotilla holidays, horse riding, fishing, wine tours, other special interests by arrangement). Ramblers Holidays, 13 Longcroft House, Fretherne Rd, Welwyn Garden City, Herts AL8 6PQ (07073 31133) (walking). Seven Seas Sailing Club, Rodmersham Green, Sittingbourne, Kent ME9 OPU (0795 71144) (flotilla and other sailing holidays). Threshold Travel, Wrendal House, 2 Whitworth St. West, Manchester M1 5WX (061 236 9763) (holidays for physically handicapped). Yugotours, 150 Regent St., London W1R 5FA (01 439 7233) (naturist, spas, historical tours, wine tours).

Transport JAT (Yugoslav Airlines), 201 Regent St., London W1 (01 734 3596); Suite 212, Rockefeller Center, 630 Fifth Ave, New York, N.Y. 10020 (212 765 4050). Thomson Holidays (Britannia Airways charter flights), Greater London House, Hampstead Rd, London NW1 7SD (01 387 2136). Jadrolinija (shipping services), Obala Jugoslavenske mornarice 16, Rijeka (051 22356). Transalpino (youth rail travel), 71/75 Buckingham Palace Rd, London SW1 (01 834 9656).

LANGUAGE

Yugoslavia has four main languages: Serbo-Croat is an umbrella name for the very similar Serbian and Croatian languages; the Slovenes and Macedonians have their own rather different languages, but all four are treated as official. The main languages of the numerous minority nationalities are Albanian, Hungarian, Slovak, Turkish, Romanian, Bulgarian, Ruthenian and Czech. In the regions where there are substantial minorities, education is provided in most of these languages, with Serbo-Croat as a compulsory subject.

The most widely spoken foreign language is German, though English is becoming an increasingly close second. More French is spoken in the centre and south than in the north and west.

The Latin alphabet is used in Croatia and Slovenia, Cyrillic in the other republics, though the Latin alphabet is generally understood there and both alphabets are used on most official signs.

Some very early examples of another

Slavonic alphabet, called Glagolitic, can be seen especially along the coast. Early Croatian literature was written in Glagolitic which also survived, despite later opposition from Rome, as the language of the church for many centuries. It was probably created in the 9th century by two Macedonian brothers, Cyril and Methodius, of whom little is known (see also under Ohrid, p. 88). From this developed the Cyrillic alphabet which spread throughout most of the Slav lands.

The pronunciation of Serbo-Croat is fairly straightforward. Each letter of the alphabet always represents the same sound and emphasis usually falls on the first syllable of a word. The table below shows the Latin alphabet with Cyrillic equivalents, and includes some notes on pronunciation.

A	А	as in c*a*lm, but very short	L	Л	as in *l*et
B	Б	as in *b*et	Lj	Љ	as 'ly' sound in pavi*li*on
C	Ц	as 'ts' in ba*ts*	M	М	as in *m*et
Ć	Ћ	as 'tsh'	N	Н	as in *n*et
Č	Ч	as 'tch' in ba*tch*	Nj	Њ	as 'ny' sound in o*ni*on
D	Д	as in re*d*	O	О	as in c*o*t
Dz	Џ	as 'j' in *j*udge	P	П	as in *p*et
Đ (Dj)	Ђ	as 'j' in *j*udge, but softer	R	Р	as in *r*ed, but rolled slightly
E	Е	as in b*e*t			
F	Ф	as in *f*og	S	С	as in *s*et
G	Г	as in *g*o	Š	Ш	as 'sh' in *sh*ut
H	Х	as 'ch' in Scottish lo*ch*	T	Т	as in be*t*
I	И	as in b*i*t	U	У	as in p*u*t
J	J	as 'y' in *y*et	V	В	as in *v*et
K	К	as in *k*ing	Z	З	as in *z*oo
			Ž	Ж	as 's' in plea*s*ure

SLOVENIA
SLOVENIJA

The northernmost of Yugoslavia's six republics, Slovenia has a population of nearly 1.9 million and covers an area of 20,251 sq km/7817 sq mi, very few of which are flat! Within relatively limited confines are packed several mountain ranges, some of the world's most remarkable caves, and a short section (about 40 km/25 mi) of the Adriatic coast. The Julian Alps are Yugoslavia's greatest mountains, the highest, Triglav, is 2863 m/9393 ft, but several others soar to over 2400 m/7870 ft. The source of the Sava, one of the country's mightiest rivers, is also to be found in these mountains. Another great range, the Karavanke, forms the border with Austria.

Slovenia provides most western visitors arriving by car with their first contact with Yugoslavia. It is the most 'sophisticated' part of the country and many Slovenes, with some justification, consider themselves a separate cultural entity. Their Slavic language is markedly different from Serbo-Croat and their history also sets them apart: from the 8th century they were ruled by a succession of Germanic kings, later becoming part of the Habsburg empire. This is strongly reflected in the Slovene style of life, from the un-

Julian Alps

mistakable architectural stamp of Central Europe in the larger towns to the neat chalet-farms in the mountains, and not least in the efficiency and know-how which has put the Slovene economy streets ahead of much of the rest of the country. All this does not mean that the people accepted foreign rule gladly. For most of the time the Slovenes were treated as a boorish peasantry speaking an archaic tongue and there were many uprisings throughout the centuries.

For a brief period Ljubljana played an important part in the struggles of the Reformation, which had one significant outcome: the birth of the Slovene printed word. Early in the 19th century Napoleon conquered the region and set up his province of Illyria with Ljubljana as capital. This gave impetus to growing national feeling and there was a minor explosion of Slovene literature, led by the poet Franc Prešern. Thereafter any further attempt to 'Germanize' the Slovenes was doomed to failure.

For visitors who know neighbouring Austria, the tidy communities nestling in Slovenia's mountains will seem very familiar, but the Slav overtones are everywhere apparent in the gastronomy, folk culture and music. An unusual and charming form of expression survives in many examples of beehive art, dating from the 18th and 19th centuries when honey was an important part of the economy. The scenes painted often depict biblical themes but also illustrate local and family life.

Slovenia produces some of Yugoslavia's best known wines as well as bottled waters from the mineral springs that account for a number of well-equipped spas. Winter sports and summer facilities are particularly well developed and, generally speaking, everything 'works' in Slovenia, variously arousing the admiration, irritation or envy of fellow Yugoslavs!

Bled D5

(pop. 5000) One of the most familiar picture-postcard views of Yugoslavia is of little lake Bled with the resort clustered beneath the castle on its eastern shore and the church-crowned islet rising out of its waters. At 501m/1643ft, this is the most popular resort in the Julian Alps whose peaks provide a magnificent backdrop as well as marvellous opportunities for walking and climbing of all grades. Here, too, in a grand setting above the upper reaches of the Sava river is Yugoslavia's only (and excellent) 18-hole golf course. Bathing, boating and wind surfing are well catered for. Bled's thermal springs were responsible for its origins as a tourist centre back

in the mid-19th century, but its reputation as an exclusive resort was firmly established between the two World Wars. Acupuncture treatment is the current speciality.

The castle was founded in the 11th century and rebuilt many times, the present buildings dating from late medieval to Baroque. It offers a museum, restaurant and breathtaking views. On the islet, the Baroque church is now a religious art museum.

For shorter outings, an attractive form of local transport is the *kočija* or horse-drawn carriage; a pleasant trip is to the lovely Vintgar gorge (via the hamlets of Podhom and Zasip, about 5km/3mi). The wide horizons of the Pokljuka plateau are 18km/11mi by road and from here ascents can be made to a number of peaks in the Julian Alps, including Triglav. Interesting museums in the area include the birthplace of the Slovene poet, Prešern, at **Vrba** (about 7km/4mi), and the Apicultural Museum at **Radovljica** (8km/5mi) devoted to Slovenia's traditional occupation of beekeeping.

Following the Sava Bohinjka (one of the

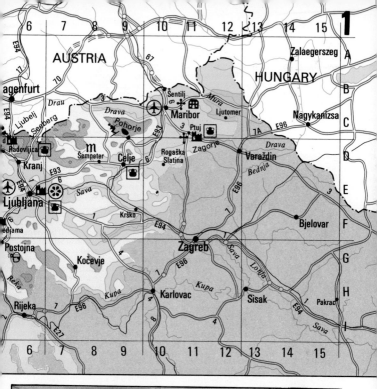

Lake Bled

upper branches of the Sava river), it is 30km/18mi south west from Bled to the resort and lake of **Bohinj** (Bohinjsko jezero) at 523m/1715ft. The resort is smaller and less sophisticated than Bled, the lake larger and in a wilder setting, with several hotels and a pretty 17th-century church on its southern shore. From road's end, about 3km/2mi beyond the Zlatorog Hotel, a steep 20-minute walk brings you up to Savica waterfall, source of the Sava

Savica waterfall in the Julian Alps

Bohinjka. From here serious walkers can continue round a chain of seven lakes (*Triglavskih jezerih*) to some of the highest Julian peaks. A cable car from near the Zlatorog Hotel brings you up on to Vogel mountain (highest point 1922m/6306ft). *Bled-Ljubljana 54km/34mi.*

Celje   D9

(pop. 37,500) Despite wartime damage, the town is interesting as the former seat of the influential Counts of Celje. Grofija, their lovely 17th-century town palace, with double arcaded courtyard, is now a history museum whose more gruesome exhibits include the skulls of the eighteen Counts. The remains of Celje castle are worth the half-hour climb for the view.

Celje's story goes back to Roman times, but the little town of **Šempeter** (12km/7½mi W) is the place to go for its open-air collection of exceptionally well-preserved or restored sarcophagi and steles from the 2nd and 3rd centuries, excavated from this once thriving Roman city of *Claudia Celeia*. There are some vivid reliefs depicting the four seasons (Priscian's tomb) and scenes such as Europa on the bull, a horse fleeing from a lion and a dog hunting a gazelle (Enius family tomb). *Ljubljana 74km/46mi.*

Kranjska Gora   C4

(pop. 1400) Only a short drive from both the Austrian and Italian frontiers, Kranjska Gora, at 810m/2657ft, is ideally placed for trips into the Julian Alps to the south (dominant peaks Prisank, 2547m/8356ft and Jalovec, 2643m/8671ft) and the Karavanke range to the north. A cable car goes up to Vitranc (1565m/5134ft).

This is one of the best-equipped skiing resorts in Yugoslavia. Being so near the borders it gets rather jammed with through-traffic in the winter and summer high seasons, but it is very easy to escape. A splendid little road leads south over the Vršič Pass to **Bovec** (44km/27mi) in the beautiful Trenta valley. *Ljubljana 88km/55mi.*

Ljubljana   E6

(pop. 303,000) The capital of Slovenia has grown from a succession of settlements on a site chosen for a good reason: it is one of the few natural breaks in the mountains that divide the Mediterranean regions from inland Europe, now known as the Ljubljana Gap. Over the ages a long line of traders and invaders have passed this way. An Illyrian settlement was followed by the Romans who first set up a military encampment before establishing the civil community of *Emona*. Most of the city's later history is closely linked with the Habsburgs, except for a brief interlude when it was the capital of Napoleon's province of Illyria.

Ljubljana is a major cultural and economic centre. It is a pleasant city on the Ljubljanica river, tucked in between the slopes of Šišenski Hrib and Castle Hill. From its hilltop eyrie, the castle affords marvellous views. Apart from the walls, which are older, most of the present structure dates from the late 15th and early 16th centuries.

The old city core clusters on the east bank of the river at the foot of the castle, its medieval aspect largely reshaped in the 17th century when it acquired its predominantly Baroque appearance. The

Old city centre, Ljubljana

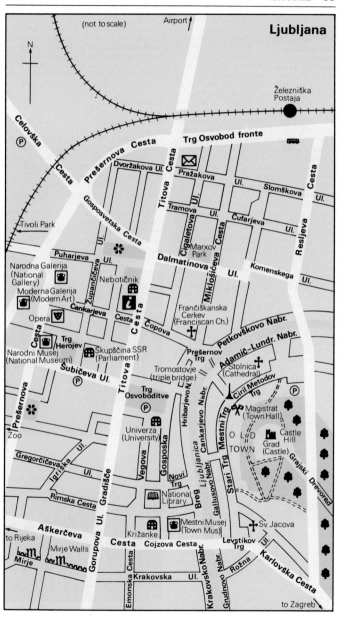

Ljubljana

focal point is Mestni trg with its fountain by Franc Robba (1751), representing the three rivers, Sava, Krka and Ljubljanica, and modelled on a Bernini fountain in Rome. The square is dominated by the Baroque Town Hall (*Rotovž*). A little to the north, on Ciril Metodov trg, the Bishop's Palace (Baroque overlays on an earlier foundation) has a fine arcaded courtyard. Next to it is the Cathedral (1700–06) with profusely decorated interior featuring statuary by Robba and epitaphs from Roman, and later, times. There is more of Robba's work in two other churches: Sv Jakova on Levstikov trg and the more handsome Frančiškanska Cerkev on Prešernov trg. The latter lies on the west bank across the river, spanned at this point by the unusual triple bridge, *Tromostovje*.

In the 17th and especially 18th centuries, the town expanded considerably over on the west bank with its shady riverside promenade (*Breg*). A few blocks west is Titova cesta, the main artery of modern Ljubljana, dominated by the 13-storey landmark, Nebotičnik building, with the tourist information office next door.

Most of the museums, galleries and the Opera House are to be found a little further west and, beyond, lie the green expanses of Tivoli Park on Šišenski Hrib. The collections of the National Museum, on Trg herojev, are especially fine and include the magnificent Vače bronze urn from the 6th century BC. Also rewarding is the Municipal Museum, on Gosposka street, housed in a 17th-century palace, a little south of the centre and adjacent to the unusual and interesting complex of Križanke. This is a 16th-century monastery built on an earlier monastic foundation of the Teutonic Order of the Knights of the Cross, which was adapted in the 1930s by Joze Plečnik as the setting for the Ljubljana Summer Festival (p. 23). A short stroll to the south west brings you to Mirje and another restoration by Plečnik: the walls marking the southern boundary of the Roman military encampment. *Zagreb 135km/84mi.*

Maribor   C10

(pop. 130,000) Only 18km/11mi from the Austrian border, Maribor straddles the Drava river. On the north bank the riverside houses and towers of the old quarters present a very pleasing picture. Hub of the town is Glavni trg with the Old Town Hall (1515) and Plague Memorial column. The Cathedral is not far to the north (founded 12th century, rebuilt 17th). South west of Maribor rise the lovely wooded Pohorje mountains (highest point

Crni Vrh, 1543m/5062ft). Though much gentler than the Slovene alps, they offer excellent winter skiing, summer rambling with many marked trails, and varied accommodation. The mountains are penetrated by minor roads and a cable car gives access to them, about 5km/3mi south west of the town centre. *Ljubljana 134km/84mi.*

Portorož   H3

(pop. 2700) This small but old-established resort of Slovenia's short (40km/25mi) stretch of coast has excellent recreational facilities. Its sheltered position, many parks and profusion of flowers – especially roses – account for its name 'port of roses'. On the headland of Seča a permanent display of modern sculpture exhibits the work of participants in 'Forma Viva', the annual international symposium of sculptors.

Of greater historical appeal are **Piran** (3km/2mi) and **Koper** (14km/9mi) to the north east, each clustered on a promontory, with narrow streets, old churches and palaces, and remains of fortifications. Piran is especially pretty and has many

Piran

associations with the Italian violinist and composer Giuseppe Tartini, born here in 1692. Koper (pop. 20,500) is much larger

15th-century loggia, Koper

and is an important rail terminal, but the old city square, Titov trg, has great charm and includes a fine Cathedral (Gothic/Renaissance with Baroque additions), 15th-century Praetor's Palace and 15th-century loggia. *Ljubljana 128km/79mi.*

Postojna G5

(pop. 6000) About 1km/½mi north west of the town centre, the magnificent Postojna Caves (*Postojnska Jama*) lie at the heart of the karst region of Slovenia. Even if you are not a cave buff, don't miss them. They form a fantastic subterranean complex of grottoes, passages and underground streams, bedecked with stalactite and stalagmite formations ranging in effect from sheer majesty to exquisite delicacy. Inscriptions show that the presence of the caves has long been known, although their full extent was not dreamed of until the 19th century. Part of the labyrinth was used as a fuel store by the Germans in World War II and blackened walls are evidence of partisan sabotage activities.

About 21km/13mi of passages and caves are open to the public on various conducted tours which begin with a 2¼km/1¼mi-long ride on a miniature railway. Dress warmly for it is very cold; cloaks are provided at the entrance if required. Many caves have names such as the Great Cathedral, Ballroom, Crystal Corridor, Crystal Hall, Concert Hall, Calvary, and some are used for concerts and other functions. Many of the formations also have names but you may prefer to let your own imagination run riot. A peculiarity are the blind fish, *Proteus anguineus*, which can be seen in a pool near the Crystal Hall. There is good accommodation near the cave entrance if you want to explore some of the many other caves in the area. At the entrance to one of them, 9km/6mi to the north west, is the impressive 16th-century castle of **Predjama**.

About 40km/25mi south west towards the coast is the famous Lippizaner stud, at

Lippizaner horse

Lipica, founded by the Austrian Archduke Charles in 1580. Riding courses are arranged here and there are daily displays by the Spanish Riding School. *Postojna-Ljubljana 53km/33mi.*

Ptuj C11

(pop. 10,600) This sturdy, picturesque and colourful little town by the Drava river has its roots in prehistory, was a Roman military settlement (*Poetovium*), and a medieval stronghold. Relics from all these periods can be seen in the castle (rebuilt 17th century) that dominates the town, or in the archaeological collections housed in the former Dominican church and monastery. The church on the main square dates from the 13th–14th centuries and its adjacent detached tower incorporates various Roman fragments. The Orpheus Monument – a Roman funeral monolith – in front of it was used as a pillory in the Middle Ages. Ptuj also has a Wine Museum, appropriate to its proximity to Slovenia's most famous vineyards (**Ljutomer** lies 33km/21mi north east). And just to the south of town lie the many attractions of **Zagorje** (p. 51). *Zagreb 120km/75mi.*

Postojna Caves

CROATIA
HRVATSKA

Croatia is the second largest of Yugoslavia's six republics, covering an area of 56,538sq km/21,823sq mi, with a population of over 4½ million. It includes part of the fertile Pannonian plains, an area of inland mountains separating plain from sea, and the lion's share of the country's fabled coastline.

The Interior The flat lands of Pannonia (originally part of the Roman province of that name) are a continuation of the great plains of Hungary and the Slav inhabitants of this region came into early conflict with their Hungarian neighbours. In 1102, the kingdom of Croatia, established nearly two centuries earlier by Tomislav, formally linked itself with Hungary by accepting Koloman as king of the Hungarians and Croats. Thereafter, it shared Hungary's fate, some of it being swallowed up by Turkey, the rest (including the capital Zagreb) submitting eventually to Habsburg rule.

The plains are interrupted by low-lying but often lovely hill country sheltering small communities whose pace and style of life seem enviably placid. Of easy access are the wooded heights of the Zagorje region north of Zagreb. South west towards the Adriatic, the mountains gain in stature and include the spectacular Plitvice lakes, south of Karlovac.

The Coast Croatia's 85 per cent share of the Yugoslav Adriatic coast totals, with all its indentations, about 1700km/1060mi, plus 725 islands, 66 of which are inhabited, and hundreds more rocks and reefs set in wonderfully clear waters reflecting a range of shades from purple and azure to palest opal. These islands are the tops of subterranean mountain ranges and many of them lie parallel to the almost continuous chain that backs the coast, their arid rocky aspect giving impressive emphasis to the changing hues of the sea and the verdant coastal fringe.

The coast can be divided roughly in two: the chunky triangle of the Istrian peninsula and the wide island-studded, relatively shallow waters of the Kvarner Gulf in the north; and the Dalmatian coast and islands with their deeper waters from Zadar south to the Montenegrin border.

Effectively cut off from the interior by mountain barriers, the history of the coast pursued its own course. A few traces survive of a number of colonies established by the Greeks from the 4th century BC. There are far more remains from Roman times (Poreč, Pula, Zadar, Split). Slav

infiltration began in the 5th century and, in the centuries following, the balance of power shifted between a miscellany of Hungarian, Serb or Bosnian rulers, an increasingly strong Venetian presence, and the local clans. Two leading names in the feudal aristocracy of those days were the Frankopans and Zrinjskis who held considerable power over the whole Kvarner area and later worked vigorously, but unsuccessfully, against the Habsburgs in the 17th century. From the early 15th century to the downfall of Venice in 1797, most of the region – with the exception of enclaves under Habsburg rule – came under Venetian rule and the 'protection' of the Lion of St Mark. Some parts did manage to retain varying degrees of independence at different times, but much of the coast was often under threat of Turkish expansion. A remarkable exception was the Republic of Ragusa (Dubrovnik) whose astonishing feats of diplomacy kept it independent for 400 years.

The architectural influence of Venice is everywhere to be seen in the exquisite little towns that cluster on promontories or beside bays along the coast and on the islands, each with its piazza-like square, bell or clock tower, municipal loggia (originally used for public trials) and collection of patrician houses. Gothic and Renaissance styles make the most typical blend.

Napoleon put an end to Venetian rule and Dubrovnik's independence at a stroke. But his attempt to establish an independent province of Illyria within his Empire lasted only a few years and, with his defeat, the coast became a further extension of the rambling Habsburg possessions. Even the reshuffle of Europe following World War I did not put an end to fragmentation for Istria, Rijeka and Zadar went to Italy and were only joined to Yugoslavia after World War II.

Island of Cres seen from Opatija

Donkeys on karst near Pečani

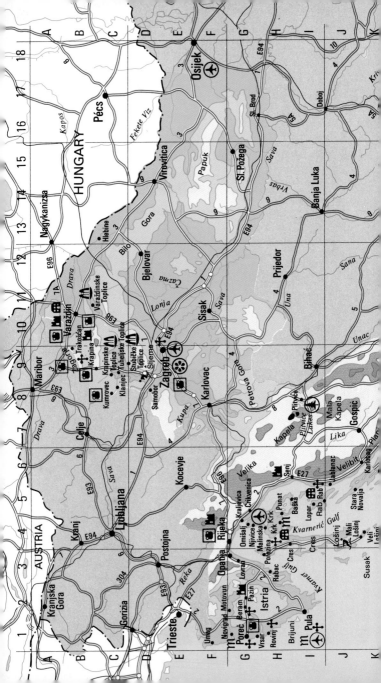

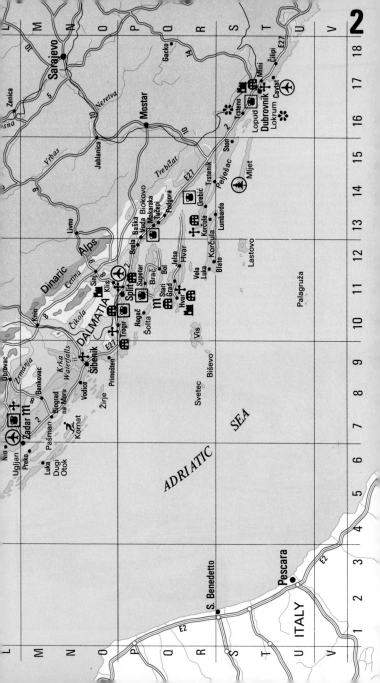

This is a marvellous coast for being as lazy or as active as temperament dictates in a setting of rare natural beauty which also provides the backdrop for an almost continuous series of summer festivals. A great additional bonus is that only a short drive across the mountains brings you to landscapes and communities reflecting totally different historical and cultural influences. Such a combination is unique in Europe.

Brač   Q11

Covering 392sq km/152sq mi, this is one of the largest of the Dalmatian islands, very rugged and largely covered, except for a few cultivated areas, by pine forests, rock and scrub. Indeed one of its main products is the mellow Brač stone used in the construction of Diocletian's Palace at Split and popular ever since. It also offers some good wines. **Supetar**, on the north coast, is the main little town, but the attractive village of **Bol**, looking across to Hvar from the south coast, is the most popular resort, with its beaches of pebbles and coarse sand. The Dominican monastery has an interesting small museum. Brač is particularly suitable for a peaceful holiday spent pottering about the rocky coastline punctuated by quiet communities, most of which house a Gothic,

Renaissance or Baroque building or two. **Ferries:** Supetar-Split, Sumratin-Makarska; also local services linking the island of Hvar via Bol-Milna-Bobovišće-Sutivan with Split.

Cres   I4

This long thin island (404sq km/156sq mi) in the Gulf of Kvarner all but touches the Istrian peninsula. A road runs its entire length from **Porozina** in the north and there is a bridge to neighbouring Lošinj to the south. It is, as yet, little developed for tourism. The main centre is **Cres** town (26km/16mi S of Porozina), a pretty place, if a little down at heel, with a number of 15th- and 16th-century buildings and fortifications dating from Venetian rule. A good choice for a quiet holiday.
Ferries: Porozina-Brestova, Porozina-Rijeka; also local services linking the islands of Lošinj, Susak, Unije via Osor-Martinščica-Cres with Rijeka.

Dubrovnik   T17

(pop. 40,500) Once in a while a place lives up to all the ecstatic descriptions. Such a place is the walled and mellow town of Dubrovnik. Originally a rocky islet, it was settled by refugees from Epidaurus (present-day Cavtat) fleeing from invading Slavs and Avars. A Slav settlement

Harbour, Cres town

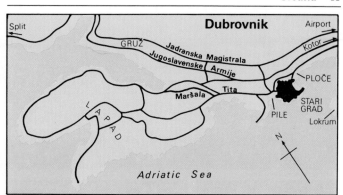

Dubrovnik

Split · GRUŽ · Jadranska Magistrala · Airport · Kotor · Jugoslavenske · Armije · PLOČE · STARI GRAD · Maršala · Tita · PILE · Lokrum · L A P A D · N

Adriatic Sea

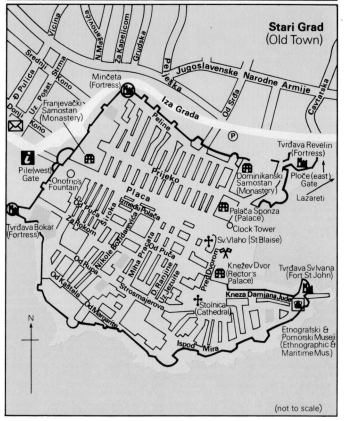

Stari Grad
(Old Town)

Split · Vicina · Stredji · Strma · Kono · Uz Posat · N.Maš · Za Kapelicom · Grudska · Jugoslavenske Narodne Armije · Cavtatska · Minčeta (Fortress) · Iza Grada · Peline · Od Srđa · Franjevački Samostan (Monastery) · Donji Kono · Pile (west) Gate · Onofrio's Fountain · Prijeko · Tvrđava Revelin (Fortress) · Dominikanski Samostan (Monastery) · Ploče (east) Gate · Lažareti · Placa · Široka · Između Polača · Palača Sponza (Palace) · Clock Tower · Tvrđava Bokar (Fortress) · Od Puča · Za Rokom · Nikole Božidarevića · Miha Pracata · Od Puča · Sv.Vlaho (St Blaise) · Od Rupe · D.Ranjine · Uz Jezuite · Pred Dvorom · Knežev Dvor (Rector's Palace) · Tvrđava Sv Ivana (Fort St John) · Od Kaštela · Strosmajerova · Kneza Damjana Jude · Od Margarite · Stolnica (Cathedral) · Etnografski & Pomorski Museji (Ethnographic & Maritime Mus.) · Ispod Mira · N

(not to scale)

Looking down on Dubrovnik

Old city walls

Rector's Palace

later developed on the mainland across a slender strait. The two settlements merged, the narrow strait was filled in (it is now the Placa or Stradun, the main thoroughfare through the old town), and the mighty walls were built. The town embarked on its remarkable history of growing maritime power and relative liberality in which literary and artistic achievement flourished (p. 9) and enlightened social reforms were made. While power struggles raged all around, the city state maintained its independence by sheer skill of diplomacy – and the payment of tribute to Turkey. It was known as Ragusa, from which comes the word 'argosy'.

Bathing in Dubrovnik is mainly off rocks or man-made bathing areas. Many of the hotels are on the peninsula of Lapad (3km/2mi, good bus service), so if you want to be within strolling distance of the walled town (closed to motorized traffic) choose a hotel in the Ploče or Pile district on either side of it.

The walls are a must. They are accessible from the Pile (west) and Ploče (east) Gates (small entrance fee), which close around dusk, and the complete circuit is nearly 2km/1¼mi. If time is short, choose the landward side for the stunning vistas of domestic roofscapes, towers, domes, spires, glimpses into monastic courtyards, tiny rooftop gardens and the amazing aerial ballet of swifts and Alpine swifts. The walls acquired their present form mainly in the 14th and 15th centuries, with later additions, and incorporate a series of towers, five bastions, two corner fortresses and, overlooking the charming old harbour from the north, massive Fort Revelin, added on in the 16th century in case diplomacy with the Turks should fail. The corner fort of St John above the south side of the harbour now contains the Ethnographic and Maritime Museums and the Aquarium. On a towering spur of rock just west of the walled city is the much restored but still formidable Fort Lovrjenac (p. 21).

Of many fine buildings within the walled city, the two most famous are the Rector's Palace (*Knežev dvor*) and the Sponza Palace. The former, a fine blend of Gothic and Renaissance with its council halls and the Rector's apartments furnished from different periods, is a fascinating museum. It also recalls the unique form of city government whereby the Rector, who headed the three councils ruling the city, resided here in luxury but isolation so that he should not be distracted from his responsibilities during the mere month of his term of office. The Sponza Palace from the same period houses the City Archives where you can peruse some of the remarkable documents from rulers of all the great powers – including British, French, Spanish, Russian and Turkish royalty – endorsing the Republic's independence

Ploče beach

Street in old town

over the centuries. One of the last is from Napoleon who less than a year later, in 1806, sent in his forces, effectively ending the Republic, which subsequently passed to Austria in 1815.

Among other fine sights are the beautiful cloisters of the Franciscan and Dominican Monasteries, the former sheltering one of Europe's earliest pharmacies. Both churches were rebuilt following damage by earthquake. Dubrovnik had its fair share of earthquakes, the most violent being in 1667, and many buildings date from the subsequent restoration, including the Cathedral (very rich treasury) and Church of Sv Vlaho (St Blaise, the city's patron saint) where a 15th-century silver statuette of the saint holding a model of old Dubrovnik stands on the main altar.

Most of the buildings along Placa and its steep narrow tributary alleys post-date the 1667 earthquake, but the 16-sided Onofrio fountain at the Pile end is from 1444 and marks one of the terminals of the old water supply system. On a nearby corner is the Dubrovnik tourist office. At the Ploče end of Placa, Orlando's Pillar was erected in 1418, the knight's forearm being used as the Republic's standard measure of length. Beside this is the Clock Tower rebuilt in its original 15th-century style in 1928 next to the bell loggia (1463, rebuilt 1952). Just outside the Ploče Gate are the old Lazarets (1590), now an attractive complex of boutiques and places of entertainment. Many of Dubrovnik's fine courtyards and squares are used for all kinds of performances in summer and especially during the Dubrovnik Festival (p. 23).

Take the cable car (or walk) to the top of Mount Srdj for fabulous views of city and coast. Uninhabited **Lokrum**, just off shore, is a popular bathing spot and protected area with botanic gardens and Institute of Biology. The inhabited Elaphite islands of **Koločep**, **Lopud** and **Šipan** have long histories and are all attractive places to spend the day. Southwards along the coast, the little resorts of **Srebreno**, **Mlini**, **Plat** and **Cavtat** (19km/12mi) are strung out along the bay – the last being the successor to the Greek, later Roman, town of Epidaurus, with Renaissance buildings and a fine mausoleum by Meštrović. Sundays are best in **Čilipi** (22km/14mi) for the costumes worn by churchgoers. North of Dubrovnik, beyond the modern harbour of Gruž, the broad inlet of the Ombla (see also p. 66) houses the Dubrovnik Marina at **Kolomac** (10km/6mi). Further north is peaceful **Trsteno** (30km/19mi) with notable botanic gardens and gigantic 400-year-old plane trees. *Zagreb 560km/348mi.*

Ferries: Dubrovnik is on express shipping routes linking Rijeka and main coastal centres, some continuing to Bar (Montenegro) and Corfu and Igoumenitsa in

Greece. Local services link Dubrovnik with the islands of Koločep, Lopud, Šipan and Mljet.

Hvar R12

A ridge runs from east to west along most of the length of this island which covers an area of 297sq km/115sq mi. Hvar is one of the loveliest and most interesting of the islands, inhabited at least 3000 years ago. The Illyrians were followed by the Greeks (the name derives from the Greek *Pharos*) and the Romans who left traces in **Stari Grad** on the north coast. One of the most interesting buildings here is the 16th-century residence of the poet Petar Hektorović, with a fishpond surrounded by a colonnade pithily inscribed in Latin or Croatian. One inscription over the lavatory states 'He who knows himself need feel no shame'.

The town of Hvar

The island's capital **Hvar** (pop. 11,200) is an architectural delight, dating mainly from Venetian rule (1420–1797). Grouped round the main square are the loggia (now part of a hotel) and adjoining Clock Tower, Cathedral, and the Arsenal through whose great arch Hvar galleons were once hauled up on to a slipway. The theatre (1612) in the adjoining building is Yugoslavia's oldest. An extensive network of fortifications sprawls up the hillside fragrant with rosemary and lavender (one of the island's main crops) to 16th-century Spagnola (Spanish Fort). North east of town, Fort Napoleon was built by the French. **Jelsa** is the main resort on the north coast (Renaissance and Baroque buildings).

Ferries: Hvar is on the express shipping route linking main coastal centres Rijeka-Dubrovnik-(Greece). Ferry services: Vira (Hvar)-Split, Sućuraj-Drvenik; also local services linking Vrboska-Jelsa with Brač island and Hvar town with Korčula island.

Karlobag K6

This small town was burnt down by the Turks, a fate also suffered by **Jablanac** (30km/19mi N). Each is overlooked by a

Jablanac, on Adriatic Highway

ruined medieval castle (Karlobag's, rebuilt by the Turks, is much more extensive) and both are linked by scenically fine roads with the interior over the Velebit mountains.

Ferries: Karlobag-Pag, Jablanac-Stara Novalja (Pag), Jablanac-Mišnjak (Rab).

Korčula R12

The enchanting island of Korčula (277sq km/107sq mi) lies to the south of Hvar, its eastern end sheltered by the long arm of the Pelješac peninsula. After changing hands many times, it submitted to Venice from 1420–1797 and most of the main monuments date from this period, many of them designed or embellished by the notable local Andrjić family. **Korčula** town (pop. 18,300), clustered on a promontory, is a real gem, the gleam of its mellow local stone visible from afar. It has been so constructed that its side streets are slightly staggered along the main street, thus creating an effective windbreak. Oft-mentioned links with Marco Polo are tenuous, but his supposed birthplace can be visited. There are old fortifications, a 17th-century triumphal arch, and plenty of Gothic, Renaissance and Baroque buildings, notably the 14th–16th-century Cathedral with an early Tintoretto of St Mark. Three religious guilds join for a major procession on Good Friday. Svi Sveti (All Saints) Church has a splendid collection of 14th–17th-century Cretan icons. See also the *Moreška* sword dance (pp. 21, 23).

A popular local excursion is to **Lumbarda** (6km/4mi SW), home of the amber-coloured Grk wine that goes straight to your knees. **Blato** is an interesting inland town. In the island's west **Vela Luka** is a quiet resort and fishing centre. Nearby islands and islets of historical interest (**Vrnik** has quarries in use since Roman times) offer pleasant bathing. See also **Pelješac** peninsula. A longer excursion is to the wooded island of **Mljet**, part of which is a national park. The 12th-century Benedictine monastery on an islet in freshwater Veliko jezero (Big

Lake) is now a hotel – a wondrously peaceful spot when the day trippers have gone.

Ferries: Korčula is on express shipping routes linking main coastal centres Rijeka-Dubrovnik-(Greece); also via Zadar to Ancona (Italy). Ferries: Korčula town-Orebić, Vela Luka-Split, Vela Luka-Lastovo island; local services link Vela Luka with Hvar and Mljet islands, and Mljet, via the Elaphite islands, with Dubrovnik.

Krk   H5
Krk lies in the Gulf of Kvarner and is Yugoslavia's largest island (411sq km/159sq mi). It is linked by a bridge to the mainland and accommodates Rijeka's airport. The main tourist centres, in or near **Baška**, **Krk** town (pop. 13,300), **Malinska**, **Njivice**, **Omišalj** and **Punat**, are mostly modern as Krk has no long tradition of tourism and is still a place for a quiet holiday. It is, however, a particularly interesting island, well worth the hire of a car to visit its many scattered sights. Krk town itself (approx. 29km/18mi from the mainland) is constantly producing more signs of its Roman origins. Among them is a Roman bath beneath a 5th-century church on top of which now stands the fine Cathedral (12th century, extended 14th-15th centuries); some of the interior columns are Roman, some from the 5th century. Thère are several Roman mosaics and very many buildings and traces of fortifications from Krk's period of glory as capital of the Frankopans (p. 36) until 1480. The Bishop's Palace is of particular interest.

The whole island is peppered with old churches and monasteries with fine paintings, wood carvings or stonework, one of the most interesting being the Monastery of **Košljun** on an islet reached from Punat. This contains a copy of the Baška tablet (original in Zagreb), one of the earliest examples of Glagolitic writing (pp. 27–8). Krk remained a staunch stronghold of the Glagolitic alphabet until recent times and there are many such inscriptions on the island.

Ferries: Šilo-Crikvenica, Baška-Senj, Baška-Lopar (Rab).

Lošinj   K4
Its 75sq km/29sq mi are linked by bridge to Cres island. Lošinj is quite unspoilt and known particularly for its mild climate (underwater fishing contests are held at New Year!) The two main communities of **Mali Lošinj** (west coast) and **Veli Lošinj** (east coast) are only 4km/2½mi apart, each clustered round a harbour. Mali Lošinj is the more developed for tourism, Veli

Lošinj prettier and older. Both offer great peace and a profusion of vegetation. Excursions by boat from Mali Lošinj go to the tiny island of **Susak**, noted for its wines and the unusual costumes with flared 'mini' skirts worn by the women at times of festivity.

Ferries: Mali Lošinj-Pula, Mali Lošinj-Zadar; local services also link Lošinj via several small islands to Cres and Rijeka.

Makarska   Q13
(pop. 17,800) This is the main resort, with excellent tourist facilities, on the fine stretch of coast known as the Makarska riviera. Its intense greenness contrasts

Makarska below Biokovo mts

with the rocky heights of the Biokovo mountains which form the immediate backdrop. Among the few historical remains is the Franciscan monastery (founded 1400, rebuilt 1614) with an impressive collection of shells from all over the world. Nearby resorts are **Baška Voda** and **Brela** (15km/9mi N) whose great pine woods are a special feature, and **Tučepi** and **Podgora** (8km/5mi S), the latter a fishing community with a great white winged monument by Radović to the founding of the Yugoslav navy. *Split 63km/39mi, Zagreb 459km/285mi.*

Ferries: Makarska-Sumratin (Brač).

Opatija   G3
(pop. 29,000) This old-established resort on the Istrian coast, only 13km/8mi from Rijeka, has a strong Central European flavour. Its sheltered position beneath the bulk of Učka mountain (1401m/4596ft) and balmy winter climate attracted a bevy of nobles and notables from the Austrian and Hungarian courts in the 19th century. Villas and inns sprang up in a rash of neo-Renaissance and neo-Baroque and the first hotel, the Kvarner (still there), was built in 1884. When development was resumed after an inter-wars slump, a new emphasis was put on summer tourism.

This stretch of riviera begins at **Volosko** (3km/2mi NE) to which Kaiser Franz Joseph brought his mistress. From its little fishing harbour, a shore path (12km/7½mi) winds all the way, via Opatija, to the much older community and quieter resort of **Lovran** (6km/4mi by road) with its narrow streets, Baroque houses and medieval tower. The coast is punctuated with small, picturesque fishing communities. A summer-long programme of events and wide range of sports facilities cater well for those who want plenty of action. About 50km/31mi south west, halfway to Pula, the attractive fishing community of **Rabac** by an inlet is another popular resort. *Ljubljana 118km/73mi.*

Pag   K6

A long, narrow, very arid island (282sq km/109sq mi), Pag lies parallel to the coastal Velebit mountains, its southern end linked by bridge to the mainland. **Pag** town, on a salt lagoon, is the most interesting centre; the 'new' town, dating from the 15th century, lies about 3km/2mi north of the ruins of Old Pag. There are a few hotels here and also at **Stara Novalja** in the north, suitable for a quiet holiday. The island is known for its wine, ewe's milk cheese, and lace.
Ferries: Pag-Karlobag, Stara Novalja-Jablanac, Stara Novalja-Mišnjak (Rab); also local ferries link Novalja with the small islands of Olib and Silba.

Pelješac peninsula   R14

This very long and narrow arm of the mainland stretches for some 70km/43mi. Its rocky landscapes produce some of Yugoslavia's best wines, notably Dingač which, though other claims are made, comes from only a few vineyards near **Trstenik**. The history of Pelješac was linked with that of the Dubrovnik Republic for nearly 500 years and the little salt-producing town of **Ston**, at the mainland end of the peninsula, is a remarkable relic from those days. An amazing complex of fortifications rambles across the nearby hillsides and the town itself contains many public buildings and monuments of bygone power, though they have been somewhat reduced by earthquake and wartime bombing. The nearby sea inlet is chequered with oyster beds. The main resort on Pelješac is **Orebić** (63km/39mi from Ston). It offers marvellous views across to Korčula and has produced an astonishing number of sea captains, many of whose fine Renaissance and Baroque houses survive. There is a maritime museum. *Ston-Split 174km/ 108mi; Ston-Dubrovnik 65km/40mi.*
Ferries: Orebić-Korčula, Trpanj-Kardeljevo, Trpanj-Drvenik, Trstenik-Polače (Mljet).

Plitvice lakes
(Plitvička jezera)   I8

The sixteen lakes and their surroundings which form the Plitvice National Park merit all the superlatives heaped upon them. Pray for good weather as the area is prone to rain and mists which also contribute to the exuberant vegetation. The lakes are cradled between richly wooded mountains, from which they are fed by a

Plitvice falls

myriad streams, and descend in a series of terraces from south to north. A drop of over 150m/500ft, between the highest lake, Prošćansko jezero, and the final plunge over the Sastavci falls into the Korana river, is achieved over a total distance of 7km/4½mi. Waterfalls range from the thunderous Sastavci falls and the double tiers of Slap Plitvice (Plitvice falls) in the same area to innumerable jaunty cascades, tumbling and chattering over the rocks. Their ceaseless and changing symphony serves only to emphasize the otherwise primeval silence. Beautiful formations of travertine (crystalline limestone) have resulted from the interaction of sediments and an exotic variety of algae and mosses. These waters contain a rich harvest, notably of trout and crayfish, both local delicacies, and in the surrounding virgin forests the trees – mostly beech and conifers – grow to tremendous size. About halfway along is a complex of modern hotels on the shores of Kozjak, largest of the lakes (boats available). Walking is the only true way of exploring the area's lush magnificence and there are plenty of marked trails. *Zagreb 139km/86mi.*

Poreč   G1

(pop, 19,900) On the west Istrian coast, Poreč combines considerable historic and architectural interest with a varied coastline and green offshore islets. This was the Roman *Parentium* and many remains include the town's layout and the Forum and Temples of Mars and Neptune. But the outstanding monument is the Basilica of Euphrasius, built in the mid-6th century on even earlier foundations. Much of the original remains, albeit restored, and major features are the interior columns, each with a different capital, some superb Byzantine mosaics in the apse, and a magnificent ciborium (1277). The old town has many fine old houses and palaces, one of which (the Baroque Sinčić Palace) contains the regional museum.

A number of modern shoreside tourist complexes are several miles away. **Vrsar** (9km/6mi S) rises up steeply from the fjord-like Limski Canal (9km/6mi long with boat trips and oyster beds). Rewarding destinations inland are **Beram** (approx. 28km/17mi) with unusually fine 15th-century frescoes in Sv Marija na Škriljinama (1km/½mi NE); **Pazin** (32km/20mi) with Istria's best medieval castle; and the charming medieval hill village of **Motovun** (approx. 30km/19mi). *Ljubljana 182km/113mi.*

Pula   I2

(pop. 77,200) The busy town and port

Roman amphitheatre, Pula

clustering round an inlet was the Roman administrative centre of Istria and splendid remains survive. The most spectacular is the huge oval amphitheatre built in the 1st century, now used for the Yugoslav Film Festival and other events. Other monuments include the Porta Gemina, Triumphal Arch, the Temple of Augustus and remnants of other temples (one of them incorporated into the partly Gothic town hall). Several churches, including the Cathedral, feature mosaics or murals and many a Roman fragment. Some miles from town are several modern tourist complexes. **Rovinj** (34km/21mi N) is a most pleasant resort and delightful old town dominated by the slender bell tower (1677) of Baroque Sv Eufemija. *Zagreb 275km/170mi.*
Ferries: Pula-Mali Lošinj-Zadar.

Rab   I5

The arid eastern aspect of the island (93sq km/36sq mi) is in great contrast to the richly green western side where the capital **Rab** (pop. 8800) is one of the prettiest towns of the entire coast. A maze of steep alleys zigzag between little squares within medieval walls beneath a distinguished miscellany of spires and towers. Most of the important buildings originated in the 12th-14th centuries and were expanded or embellished during Venetian rule. Among them is the beautiful little Romanesque Cathedral with its perfectly proportioned marble columns, carved Gothic choir stalls and probably the loveliest Romanesque bell tower on the coast. Among many noble houses bearing the crests of long-past Venetian and Slav aristocrats are the Knežev dvor (Prince's Palace, Gothic-Renaissance) and Renaissance Diminis-Nimira Palace. In one district, you can see houses with sealed doors deserted by their inhabitants during a 15th-century plague. There are modern tourist complexes in the park-like setting of **Suha Punta** (5km/3mi NW) or facing the mainland near **Lopar** (15km/9mi N). **Ferries:** Rab is on express shipping routes linking main coastal centres Rijeka-Dubrovnik-(Greece). Ferries: Mišnjak-Jablanac, Mišnjak-Stara Novalja (Pag).

Rijeka G4
(pop. 193,000) Yugoslavia's largest port is also a main industrial centre. If you need to stay, there are good museums, galleries, some medieval walls and pleasant parks. The fortress of Trsat above the town, reached by several hundred steps or by bus, gives splendid views. Though under Habsburg rule for the most part, ownership of Rijeka was long contested and, following a daring takeover by Gabrielo d'Annunzio in 1919, it became Italian (as Fiume) until 1947, divided from its Yugoslav suburb Susak by the little Rjecina river.

Rijeka marks the beginning of the Croatian littoral to the south east, including the popular resorts of Kraljevica (24km/15mi) and Crikvenica (39km/24mi, ferry to Krk island); and the Istrian riviera to the west (see Opatija). *Zagreb 172km/107mi.*
Ferries: Rijeka is the main terminal for all express coastal routes linking main centres the length of the coast. Ferries: Rijeka-Porozina (Cres); also local services to other centres on Cres, Lošinj and smaller Kvarner islands.

Senj H6
This fascinating little place was the historic stronghold of the bellicose Uskoks, Slav refugees from the Turks. Though ostensibly manning a Habsburg bastion against the Turks in the 16th century, the Uskoks also took to the sea and mercilessly harried the Venetian fleets for nearly 200 years until Austria was finally forced to disband them and resettle them elsewhere. Fortifications, churches and palaces date from those and earlier times, and many folk songs record the exploits that earned the Uskoks a fearsome reputation. A splendid road leads over the Vratnik Pass through the Velebit mountains and eventually comes to the Plitvice lakes (89km/55mi). *Zagreb 159km/99mi.*
Ferries: Senj-Baška (Krk); Senj-Lopar (Rab).

Šibenik O9
(pop. 80,100) Situated on the twisting Krka estuary, Šibenik is an old Dalmatian town. It was fortified against many Turkish attacks during Venetian rule (1412–1797). Scores of decorated doorways tell of the feuds and achievements of

Šibenik's noble families and there are many decorated wells. The stone and marble Cathedral in Gothic-Renaissance style is one of the noblest buildings on the coast, and is largely the work of Juraj Dalmatinac and Nicholas of Florence. Its famous exterior frieze features 74 portrait heads of astonishing variety. Note especially the baptistry (1452, superb ceiling and amusing font). The **Krka waterfalls** (approx. 27km/17mi) are a famous local beauty spot from which boat trips go to Visovac Monastery (art collection) on an island in a lake. Two attractive seaside resorts have developed round the fishing communities of **Primošten** (17km/11mi S) and **Vodice** (13km/8mi W). *Zagreb 348km/216mi.*
Ferries: local services to Vodice and several islands (Zlarin, Kaprije, Žirje, *etc*).

Split P11
(pop. 235,900) A major industrial centre and port, Split is linked by air, rail, road and sea to the four corners of Yugoslavia. Yet even today Diocletian, the Illyrian emperor of Rome (AD 284–305), would still find familiar landmarks in the old city huddled within the walls of the magnificent palace built for his retirement. Here, in the 7th century, refugees from the once important city of Salona (now scattered ruins in the countryside to the north west) sought shelter from the invading Slavs and Avars. When the Slavs took over, a prospering medieval city expanded beyond the palace walls. The 15th century brought the protection of Venice and expanding fortifications against the Turkish threat; Habsburg rule followed from 1797. The main sights are within the palace rectangle (approx. 218m/718ft by 176m/580ft) and the adjoining medieval city. Three of the four city gates are still in use.

The palace once rose from the sea, but is now separated from it by the broad street of Titova Obala where, at No. 12, you will find the tourist office. The Underground Halls of the palace, now cleared of centuries of rubbish, reflect the original layout. Robert Adam, the Scottish architect, spent several weeks here in 1757 ferreting among the debris (to the alarm of the authorities) and published his findings which are echoed in many of his buildings in Britain. From the Underground Halls, steps lead up to the Peristyle, once the focus of palace ceremonies, with its columns (on the west side incorporated into a row of Gothic and Baroque houses), Egyptian sphinx, circular Vestibulum (a shell of the entrance hall to the Emperor's private rooms) and, above all, the Cathed-

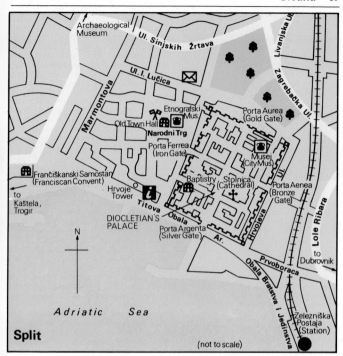

Split (not to scale)

Adriatic Sea

ral. This splendid building evolved from Diocletian's mausoleum, whose octagonal main structure is almost unchanged. Outstanding features include the superb wooden door with 28 panels depicting the life of Christ (1214), 13th-century carved choir stalls, and a beautiful relief by Dalmatinac (1448) on the altar of St Anastasius. From the Peristyle, narrow Kraj Sveti Ivana leads to the Baptistry (barrel-vaulted coffered ceiling) in what was probably part of a temple of Jupiter.

The narrow streets are packed with interesting architectural detail and Gothic and Renaissance palaces, one of which (Papalić Palace) houses the excellent City Museum. From the palace area, Porta Ferrea (Iron Gate) leads west into the medieval city with its main hub of Narodni trg. The 15th-century Old Town Hall (now Ethnographic Museum) is here, and there are more narrow streets, palaces, churches and chapels to discover.

To the west of the old town, take the waterfront road round the Marjan peninsula for the Meštrović Gallery (2km/1¼mi), former home of this great

sculptor, and, a little further, the 17th-century villa Kastelet (fine wooden reliefs by Meštrović in the chapel). By the main road, you reach the superb little town of **Trogir** (27km/17mi) but it is worth taking the longer coastal road through several small communities, known collectively as **Kaštela**, each of which developed round a feudal stronghold built as defence against the Turks. Trogir, linked by bridge to the mainland, is like a stage set. It was originally settled by the Greeks, but reached its peak of prosperity in the 12th-13th centuries, prior to Venetian rule. Its outstanding monument is the Romanesque-Gothic Cathedral with fabulous west portal by Radovan (1240), Gothic choir stalls, a chapel with coffered ceiling in the north aisle by Nicholas of Florence, valuable paintings and treasury. Several notable 15th-century buildings (Town Hall, city loggia, clock tower, Cipiko Palaces) stand around the main square, Narodni trg.

An interesting inland excursion is to the fortress of **Klis** (12km/7mi), a major stronghold in the struggle between Venice

Diocletian's Palace, Split

and Turkey, and **Sinj** (34km/21mi), scene of the spectacular *Alka* pageant (pp. 21, 24). *Zagreb 396km/246mi.*

Ferries: Split is on the express shipping route linking main coastal centres Rijeka-Dubrovnik-(Greece); also via Zadar to Ancona. Ferries: Split-Supetar (Brač), Split-Vira (Hvar), Split-Stari Grad (Hvar), Split-Rogač (Šolta); also local services linking Split with Trogir and communities on the islands of Brač, Drvenik Mali, Drvenik Veli, Hvar, Korčula and Šolta.

Trogir

Umag   F1
Both Umag and smaller **Novigrad** (16km/10mi S) cluster prettily on promontories on the west Istrian coast. Both have medieval and later monuments, and modern tourist complexes in the neighbourhood. *Ljubljana 146km/91mi.*

Varaždin   B10
(pop. 90,700) It is worth overcoming first impressions of this rather drab industrial town on the Drava river. Its chief sight is the castle, originally 13th century but strongly fortified in the 16th against the

Turks, now housing a history museum. The Town Hall dates from 1523 but most of the charming, if at times dilapidated, palaces in the centre are from the 17th and 18th centuries. Some past owners are commemorated by lavishly ornate tombstones and mausoleums set among fine topiary in Varaždin's cemetery, modelled rather surprisingly on the park of Versailles. The spa waters of **Varaždinske Toplice** (15km/9mi S) were known in Roman times. Many of the sights described under Zagorje are also easily reached from here. *Zagreb 77km/48mi.*

Zadar   M6
(pop. 116,100) The economic and traffic hub of northern Dalmatia stands on a peninsula of the coastal plain of Ravni Kotar. Most of the hotels are in the neighbouring district of Borik (5km/3mi). Zadar's pleasantly modern aspect is largely due to the post-war rebuilding which belies its great age. Roman remains, especially, are scattered but impressive. The Roman Forum, just a block from the quayside of Obala Maršala Tita, is approx. 94m/309ft long by 44½m/146ft wide, with liberal fragments and foundations of colonnades, shops, a triumphal arch and basilica. Soaring above it is Zadar's most famous landmark, the church of Sv Donat from the 9th century, remarkable not only for its age and size but for the extraordinary jumble of Roman fragments embedded in its structure. North of it is the magnificent Romanesque Cathedral of Sv Stošija (Anastasia), mainly from the 12th-13th centuries but incorporating parts of an earlier church; the west front is beautiful. About a dozen other ancient churches survive in various states of repair (several showing signs of Roman stonework). Romanesque Sv Krševan is of special note.

Most of the medieval fortifications, expanded during Venetian rule, were later pulled down but there is a substantial section in the eastern part of town overlooking the pretty little port of Foša. Also in this area is Trg Pet Bunara with five 16th-century well heads, part of the water supply system created when Turkish invasion threatened. The tower of Bablja Kula beside them is a remnant of the earlier medieval fortifications and nearby is the most impressive of several gates, the Town Land Gate (1543) still in use. The Archaeological Museum, Historical Archives and Ethnographic Museum are all worth visiting.

The scattered ruins and tumbled masonry of **Nin** (18km/11mi N) mark the once prosperous Roman *Aenona*, later

Croatian *Nona*, abandoned and destroyed in the 17th century. It was the seat of 11th-century Bishop Gregory, champion of Slavonic liturgy. From Novigradsko More (Novigrad Sea), a great enclosed bay to the north east of Zadar, boat trips are arranged up the dramatic Zrmanja Canyon to the colourful little town of **Obrovac**. Narrow straits divide Zadar from **Ugljan** and **Pašman** islands (good for quiet holidays); boat trips further afield are recommended to the strange, little-known Kornat islands. Most of them are uninhabited and have been sculpted by wind and soil erosion into bizarre contours. They are marvellous for underwater swimming and will suit those in search of a rugged solitude. *Zagreb 337km/209mi.*

Ferries: Zadar is on express shipping routes linking main coastal centres Rijeka-Dubrovnik-(Greece); also Zadar-Ancona and Zadar-Silba-Mali Lošinj-Pula. Ferries: Zadar-Preko (Ugljan); also local services to many little-known islands (Iž, Dugi Otok, Molat, Ist, Silba, Olib, *etc*).

Zagorje   B9

This most attractive region of rolling hills and fertile valleys lies north of Zagreb (from which all distances are given). From the main Zagreb-Maribor road side roads of varying standards lead to a host of interesting or charming little places (ancient castles, old churches, small spas) through orchards and vineyards and past typical Zagorje-style farmsteads of timber and whitewash. A feature of each vineyard is the *klet*, a small shack for storing wine and the focus of family festivities on summer evenings.

A famous place of modern pilgrimage is the small, typical Zagorje community of **Kumrovec** (62km/39mi), where Tito's childhood home is now a museum. His statue in the garden is by Antun Augustinčić whose home was in nearby **Klanjec**. Two small spas in this part of Zagorje are **Krapinske Toplice** (50km/31mi) and **Tuheljske Toplice** (48km/30mi), the latter offering extensive recreational facilities.

Tucked away in the lovely Ivanšcica hills, east of the main road, is **Belec** (68km/42mi), a rural gem with two churches. One from the 13th century is attached to the ruined castle while, down the hill, the other is an opulent extravaganza in Baroque and Rococo, commissioned by a countess after a vision.

Just off the main road in a narrow gap between the hills is **Krapina** (61km/38mi) whose claim to fame lies in the discovery here of *homo krapiniensis*, in 1899. The remains of this 150,000-year-old Neanderthal man now lie in Zagreb but, on a hillside near the town, an open-air museum recreates Neolithic life. Above the main road is the lovely Baroque Marija Jerusalemska church with arcaded courtyard.

The whole of the Zagorje is peppered with medieval castles, the finest of which is probably **Trakošćan** (82km/51mi), now a museum in a fine lakeside setting. Lose yourself in the Zagorje byways and you are guaranteed to make your own discoveries.

Trakošćan Castle

Zagreb D9

(pop. 1,600,000) Capital of Croatia, leading industrial, commercial and cultural centre, site of major international trade fairs, Zagreb has a fine situation by the Sava river at the foot of Mount Medvednica (or Sljeme, 1035m/3395ft). It is a handsome city with the unmistakable architectural stamp of Central Europe, offering some of the country's most interesting museums and a bustling, cosmopolitan character.

The tourist information centre, 14 Zrinjevac, can tell you what's on and where, and from here you are well placed to start exploring. The city divides itself naturally into two areas: the old Upper Town and newer, expanding Lower Town. The former is, of course, the more aesthetically pleasing and actually developed in two quite separate parts: *Grič* or Gradec (today's Gornji Grad or Upper Town), proclaimed a sovereign royal town by Hungarian Bela IV in 1242; and *Kaptol* round the Cathedral at its foot, whose development was somewhat stifled as a dependence of the Church. The Upper and Lower Towns are linked in under a minute by an ancient funicular, much beloved of Zagreb's citizens, but it is also worth the climb through the narrow streets where most of the city's oldest buildings survive.

St Mark in the Upper Town

The Turks never entered Zagreb, but it was the Turkish threat that prompted the fortifications of Kaptol in the 15th century, parts of which can be seen round the Cathedral. Fortifications surrounding Grič date from the 13th century when Bela IV took refuge here following the Tartar threat. Lotršćak Tower, from which a cannon is fired each noon, and Kamenita vrata (Stone Gate) are remnants from the same period. A shrine has blossomed in the shelter of the latter bearing countless small tablets simply inscribed 'thank you' in many languages. The Upper Town is still lit by gas lamps by a man who goes round each evening (on a motorbike!) The main church is Sv Marka (St Mark), much restored since the 13th century and containing sculptures by Meštrović, including a fine Crucifix. The colourful roof depicting various coats of arms dates from the 19th century. The Cathedral, too, was first built in the 13th century and entirely rebuilt in its present neo-Gothic style in the 19th century. The Baroque church of Sv Katerine (1632) shows least change. Many a palace dates from the 17th and 18th centuries, a time when, with the Turkish threat removed, the aristocrats of this then Hungarian province began to build their winter palaces in and around the city. Today they house various institutions, museums and art galleries.

Close to the Cathedral is the square of Dolac where a bustling and very varied market flourishes seven days a week. From here it is a stone's throw to Trg Republike, the heart of the modern city with the main street of Ilica (full of shops) going west and a series of streets, known locally as Zrinjevac, leading south to the railway station, the Sava river and, beyond it, the exhibition grounds. Most of the district between these two major arteries dates from around the turn of the century and here you will find many of the main museums, galleries, theatres and travel agencies.

Among the many museums, excellent in their own field, are the Archaeological, Ethnographic and Zagreb City Museums. The Strossmayer Gallery of Old Masters is Yugoslavia's largest collection, while the Gallery of Primitive Art provides a good introduction to the colourful works of Croatia's naive painters. The Meštrović Gallery is dedicated to Yugoslavia's most famous sculptor.

For a rest from city streets, go to Maksimir Park, a great green wooded lung north east of the centre, where you can walk for hours in what were once royal hunting grounds. Beyond this you are on the slopes of Medvednica; the top is accessible by cable car from Gračani district (tram nos. 14 and 21). There are many attractive restaurants in this leafy district on the way to the extensive rolling hills that form a natural summer and winter playground for Zagreb's citizens. *Belgrade 389km/242mi.*

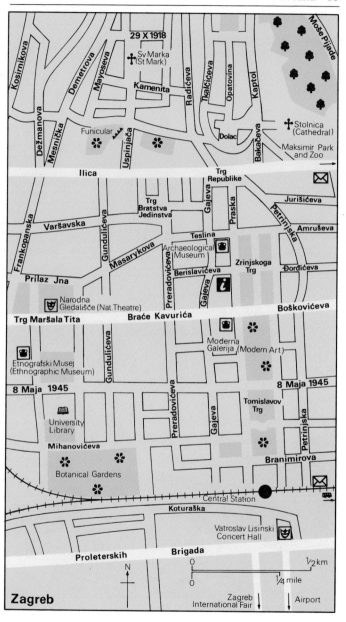

Zagreb

The Cathedral, Zagreb

BOSNIA-HERZEGOVINA

BOSNA I HERCEGOVINA

If ever East meets West it is here among the magnificent mineral-rich mountains of Yugoslavia's central republic. Bosnia-Herzegovina covers an area of 51,129sq km/19,747sq mi, has a population of about 4¼ million and is almost landlocked. The coastal strip, around the port of Kardeljevo, is only 22km/14mi long. The mountains are threaded by deep ravines or broken by fertile plateaus where sheep farming predominates; but there is a dramatic difference between the verdant, often deeply-wooded ranges of Bosnia in the north and the dry, pale wine- and tobacco-producing karst of Herzegovina in the south. The two are divided by a watershed, the streams on one side eventually tumbling into the Danube thence to the Black Sea and, on the other side, feeding the Neretva on its way to the Adriatic.

An independent state developed in the late 12th century under King Kulin and around this time the region became a stronghold of what some experts identify as Bogomilism, a heretic sect (meaning 'beloved of God') whose origins are still shrouded in mystery. It was probably founded by a 10th-century Bulgarian priest, spreading via Macedonia to Bosnia and much further afield even to France and England. Bogomilism is related to other dualistic heretic movements – especially the Manichee – who believed the Devil to be the creator of the material world and therefore that all material goods and things of the flesh should be shunned. Paradoxically, the chief evidence of their strong presence survives in the very many extremely solid tombstones (*stećci*, singular *stećak*) scattered about the countryside.

In 1463, the Turks overran Bosnia and a few years later Herzegovina. They offered protection to the Bogomils and perhaps because of this many were converted to Islam (there are over 1,600,000 Moslems in the republic today). There followed a period of economic stagnation that lasted over four centuries, though it left the region with a rich heritage of Islamic art and architecture, and the merging of East-West influences is very marked in the folk culture. The novels of Nobel Prize winner Ivo Andrić give an excellent picture of those times.

The Bosnian nationalist movement gained impetus in the late 19th century following Serbia's independence (p. 67). Uprisings supported by Serbia, Montenegro and the Slav might of Russia in the 1870s ended at last in victory, though the result was hardly what the Bosnians had anticipated. By the Congress of Berlin of 1878, Austria-Hungary was given a mandate to administer the republic and in 1908 arbitrarily annexed it completely. Nationalist fervour boomed. One consequence was the forming of Mlada Bosna (Young Bosnia), a secret society of university students whose activities – supported by Serbia to a degree that is still the subject of dispute – culminated in the assassination by the youthful Gavrilo Princip of the Austrian Archduke Franz Ferdinand in Sarajevo on 28 June, 1914. In a headlong rush of events that no diplomacy seemed able to control, the great powers rattled their sabres, amassed their armies and launched themselves into the holocaust of World War I.

During World War II, the mountains of Bosnia-Herzegovina were a stronghold of partisan activity, and the birth of the Socialist Republic of Yugoslavia was first declared on Bosnian soil at Jajce in 1943, almost under the nose of the enemy. Since the 1950s, industrialization, improved communications and an epidemic of modern building have projected Bosnia-Herzegovina virtually from the feudal to the technological age in a few decades. For many visitors, it is a transit region between the big inland cities and the coast. Yet scenically, culturally and historically it is immensely rewarding. The slender minaret is a predominant feature but may often share the skyline with Orthodox domes or towers or the occasional Catholic spire. Characteristic domestic architecture is seen in houses with whitewashed walls beneath high steep roofs of

56

black wooden tiles. The flavour of the Orient is strong in the market place, in the sound of music, in the costumes and crafts. Local variations are many, but the male fez and loose breeches or the long voluminous bloomers of Moslem women are still a common sight. Beautifully woven carpets and the art of the copper- and silversmith are an intrinsic part of the bazaar scene. In any of the innumerable little eating places called *aščinica* you can nibble the tasty *burek* (p. 18) or sweet-meats of indisputable Turkish origin, and you'll probably never drink finer Turkish coffee than here. Away from the main towns, it is still very much a male-dominated society, so that the contrasts offered by the discos now proliferating in such places as Sarajevo make an even greater impact.

There are good road and rail connections in most directions, but it is still very easy to escape from the 1980s. Walking, fishing, kayaking and hunting are all activities well catered for if you contact the appropriate local organizations.

Banja Luka   E6
(pop. 183,600) The Romans had a military camp at this crossing point of the swift Vrbas river and established a spa by the mineral springs of Gornji Šeher, which are still in use 3km/2mi upstream. The town gained great importance under Turkish rule when the fortress was built (16th century) and for a time was the seat of the Supreme Bey. The Ferhadija mosque and, opposite it, the Sahat Kula (clock tower) also date from this time. The older and more picturesque part of town is on the left bank and you will find here many examples of typical Bosnian architecture. But modern districts have grown apace, especially since a violent earthquake in 1969. On Šehitluci hill, above Gornji Šeher, the great white war memorial by Augustinčić seems about to soar into the skies. *Zagreb 186km/116mi.*

Bihać   E1
(pop. 65,500) A great many finds from prehistoric, Roman and medieval times have been made in or near this ancient town on the Una river. Some of them can be seen in the Regional Museum. There are also remains of the medieval castle and fortifications. The Fethija mosque, adapted from a Gothic church in 1592, is of interest and numerous Moslem cemeteries are a feature of the area. *Zagreb 146km/91mi.*

Čapljina   M8
(pop. 26,000) This small town by the swift green Neretva river is well sited for

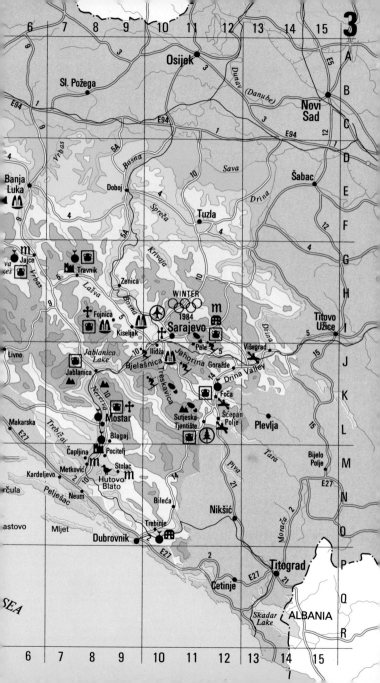

Počitelj by Neretva river

visiting several unusual places of interest. The town is modern, but across the river and about 3km/2mi north, right beside the main road to the coast, is ancient **Počitelj**, a village dating mainly from the Turkish period. It lay virtually deserted and in ruins until recently when it was restored and turned into an artists' colony. A medieval castle, 17th-century fortifications, a mosque, an old *han* (inn) and many venerable houses pile up against the hillside above the river, providing accommodation and a restaurant in a delightful if slightly contrived setting. Foreign artists can apply to stay here.

About 20km/12mi to the south east in the heart of rugged karst country is the impressive cemetery of Radimlja, near the small town of **Stolac**, with some of the best examples of Bogomil *stećci* (p. 55). Other points of interest near Čapljina are the ruins of a Roman villa at Mogorjelo (1½km/1mi S), and the extensive water wilderness and hunting reserve of **Hutovo Blato**, beginning about 8km/5mi to the south east. It is alive with wildfowl in winter, but you will need a

boat and guide to get the full benefit. *Mostar 29km/18mi.*

Drina valley   J12

Though much of the magnificent turbulence of this river has been tamed into a long curving lake in its lower stages, the upper reaches are still among the most remarkable stretches of Yugoslavia's many remarkable waterways. The river is born at the confluence of the Tara (p. 86) and Piva near **Šćepan Polje** on the Montenegrin border and then continues on a helter-skelter course through scenery of great grandeur to **Foča**, **Goražde** and **Višegrad** (a total distance of nearly 100km/62mi) beyond which the 50km/31mi-long lake begins. Just to the west of the uppermost reaches is the **Sutjeska-Tjentište National Park**, centred round a deep valley in Bosnia's highest mountains (Maglić 2386m/7828ft, Zelengora 2015m/6611ft) fed by the Sutjeska river as it rushes down to join the Drina. The park has accommodation and sports facilities, and marked trails lead to some of its wildest beauty, including the

Gorge on Neretva river

primeval forest of Perućica. These landscapes were the setting for some of the partisans' most legendary battles in World War II, commemorated by a museum and mausoleum.

Rafting trips have long been a special feature of the Drina valley, especially between Foča and Višegrad and, by prior arrangement, from Šćepan Polje. Foča is an interesting little town whose relics from Turkish times include the Aladža mosque (1551), an 18th-century inn (now restaurant), and the Prijeka bazaar with typical workshops. It was also the headquarters of Tito's Supreme Command in 1942 and has a museum to those times. Goražde is of less interest, but Višegrad can claim one of Yugoslavia's most famous structures: the stone bridge over the Drina, 175.5m/575ft in length with eleven arches. Though badly damaged in both World Wars, it has been restored to its original form, complete with the texts testifying that it was built in 1571–7. The story of its building and the conflicts it witnessed in the following centuries are the theme of Nobel Prize winner Ivo Andrić's splendid novel *The Bridge on the Drina*. Boat trips through wild scenery can be arranged on the artificial lake created by the Drina below Višegrad. *Višegrad-Belgrade 258km/160mi.*

Jablanica J8

(pop. 11,900) This is a pleasant halt on the way from Sarajevo to Mostar and a launching pad for excursions into the Prenj and Čvrsnica mountains which rise to over 2000m/6560ft; the latter offer some exacting rock climbs. These mountain ranges are separated by a particularly wild ravine created by the Neretva river and pursued by the main road to the south of the town. The town itself is situated near the man-made 30km/19mi-long Jablaničko jezero (lake) and is famed in Yugoslav annals for partisan action which saved thousands of lives during the Second World War when a bridge was built overnight across the tempestuous Neretva. A memorial museum complex graphically recalls the events. *Sarajevo 82km/51mi.*

Jajce

Jajce   G6

(pop. 41,200) Its setting is the photographer's delight. The historic core of the town piles up a hill at the foot of which the Pliva river crashes down impressive waterfalls to join the Vrbas. The town has a long story: a temple dedicated to Mithras remains from Roman times, and the Illyrians had a settlement before that. It was the seat of Bosnian kings in the 15th century but finally yielded to the Turks after a long siege in 1527, the last Bosnian stronghold to succumb, its importance dwindling as Sarajevo's increased.

There are many remains of old fortifications, several mosques and some fine examples of houses in old Bosnian style. The tower of St Luke is probably from the 14th century. A curious if dank shrine is the 15th-century family crypt of Hrvoje Vukčić with Bogomil symbols on the main altar. On 29 November, 1943, Jajce leapt into history again when, with war still raging, Tito and his National Liberation Congress proclaimed the birth of the new Socialist Republic of Yugoslavia. There is, of course, a museum in the hall where this momentous meeting took place. The Pliva lakes (13km/8mi W) have good recreational facilities. On the way you pass a most venerable group of wooden watermills, some 200 years or more old, powered by a shallow waterfall. *Zagreb 258km/160mi.*

Gate in city wall, Jajce

Watermills on banks of Pliva river

16th-century Turkish bridge, Mostar

Mostar   **L8**

(pop. 110,300) Straddling the Neretva river after it emerges from one of its many gorges, Mostar is set in a broad basin amidst pale, arid karst hills which nevertheless shelter vines and good crops of tobacco. It is known as Yugoslavia's warmest town in summer and coldest in winter. The most famous sight in this pleasant capital of Herzegovina is the old bridge over the Neretva: a beautiful, steeply angled, single-span structure built in 1566 and rising to 20m/65ft above the river; from its highest point the male youth of the town prove their manhood by jumping or diving into the swift, ice-green waters below (there is even a competition every 4 July). The bridge is guarded at each end by a 17th-century gate tower. The oldest and most picturesque part of town is centred round this bridge and Kujundžiluk, the narrow street above the left bank, linking the bridge with Karadžozbeg mosque (1557). The once rather dilapidated charms of this district have been tidied up, perhaps losing a little in the process, though it is full of small shops, craft workshops and typical restaurants, one of which has a terrace right over the river. The modern main shopping district is on the right bank and of less interest. Karadžozbeg is the most interesting of Mostar's many mosques with carpets donated by Moslem heads of state and a 600-year-old copy of the Koran. But, as in many other towns in this republic, minarets share the Mostar skyline with Orthodox towers and even Catholic spires. The old Orthodox church is on the eastern side of town.

The most interesting collections are in the History and Ethnographic Museum,

Old Turkish quarter, Mostar

Carpets for sale

housed in a mosque near the old bridge. Another museum building is Bišćevića Ćošak, an excellent example of Turkish-local architecture, furnished in original style. The 20th century has contributed more in quantity than in elegance. There is, however, a very fine war cemetery and monument by Bogdanović, which creates a cascade of stone above the north west of the town.

The Buna river tumbles into the Neretva about 10km/6mi south of Mostar, and a minor road leads south east through the little town of **Blagaj** to the source of the Buna, gushing dramatically from a sheer sheet of rock, watched over by the remains of a Dervish monastery. This rock face is crowned by the substantial ruins of medieval Blagaj including the castle of Herceg (Duke) Stefan Kosača who gave Herzegovina its name. The

Buna also powers some old watermills, still in operation, and the area is a marvellous haunt for fishermen. It is also the home of the award-winning Žilavka and Blatina wines which were once supplied to the Habsburg court. *Sarajevo 130km/ 81mi.*

Neum   N8
This modern town is Bosnia-Herzegovina's only seaside resort on the republic's short (22km/14mi) stretch of coast, which also accommodates the port of **Kardeljevo** at the mouth of the Neretva. Neum is on the Adriatic Highway, facing the long rugged arm of the Pelješac peninsula (p. 46) across a narrow sea inlet. *Sarajevo 205km/137mi.*
Ferries: Kardeljevo is linked by sea via Korčula-Zadar to Ancona (Italy). Ferries: Kardeljevo-Trpanj (Pelješac).

Sarajevo I11

(pop. 447,000) One of the most interesting places in Yugoslavia, Sarajevo is the capital of Bosnia-Herzegovina, a major industrial and cultural centre, and venue of the 1984 Winter Olympics. It sits at the heart of some of the wildest landscapes in Europe: mountain ranges with great deep forests ribbed by ravines and valleys sheltering a rural way of life that is unaffected by modern technology. A city with its back to the mountains, it spills down the lower slopes and along the narrow space afforded by the little Miljacka river on its way to join the upper reaches of the Bosna.

Such, however, has been the pace of recent growth that first you must penetrate highrise suburbs and the great modern blocks of the city's enterprises and institutions. Next, stretching east from the railway station and the National Museum, you come to solid Central European structures built during Habsburg rule from 1878 to World War I. These buildings incorporate certain oriental elements that find no echo in Zagreb or Belgrade. Finally, right up against the mountains, you reach the old Turkish centre of what was originally called *Sarajovasi* (meaning Plain around the Palace). Turkish rule dates from 1435. What you see today is what has survived flood, fire and, in particular, devastation by the army of Prince Eugène of Savoy (p. 67); but there is no shortage of sights.

Four parallel streets cross the 'Habsburg' centre of town to converge on the heart of the Turkish district. They are Maršala Tita, Vase Miskina, Jugoslavenske Narodne Armije (JNA) and Obala Vojvode (along the Miljacka river). On or near these streets are most of the shops, museums, hotels, restaurants and, at JNA 50, the tourist information office. This is only a short stroll from the place everyone wants to see: Baščaršija, the old bazaar, which has been tidied up over recent years but still has its higgledy-piggledy rows of tiny shops whose double-shuttered doors stand open to reveal craftsman and merchant (sometimes one and the same) at your service. Some scores of traditional crafts are still practised and whole streets are dedicated to the skills of the coppersmith, goldsmith, saddler and blacksmith. This is the place to buy filigree or slippers or even a finely-worked set of tiny coffee cups if you think you will ever make use of it. Interspersed are *aščinica* serving spicy local specialities or, increasingly, cafédiscos which are as noisy and full of the young as anywhere else. Many of the city's most interesting buildings are to be found amidst this maze. A number of them were founded during the rather enlightened

Turkish metalwork, Sarajevo

rule of Gazi Husref-Bey (1521–41). They include Sarajevo's finest mosque and the *medresa* (religious school) facing it, the *hamam* (public baths, now a night club), *bezistan* (warehouse, now commercial premises), and library, all bearing his name. Next to the mosque is the 17th-century Sahat Kula (clock tower) with Arabic numerals recording the twelve hours between sunrise and sunset. Another old warehouse, Brusa Bezistan, now houses a handicrafts exhibition and shops,

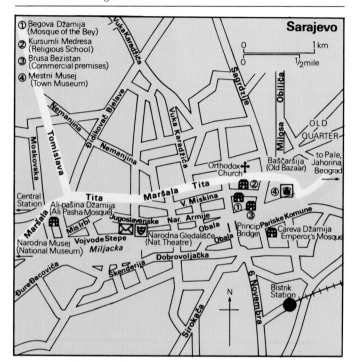

① Begova Džamija
  (Mosque of the Bey)
② Kursumli Medresa
  (Religious School)
③ Brusa Bezistan
  (Commercial premises)
④ Mestni Musej
  (Town Museum)

Sarajevo

while a third contains the excellent traditional restaurant, Daira. Many visitors
venture no further than the Baščaršija
area, but up on the hillside, near ancient
cemeteries of Jew and Moslem, you can sit
outside unpretentious small cafés looking
down on the amazing sprawl of the city.

The Ali Pasha mosque (Ali-pašina
džamija) and Emperor mosque (Careva
džamija) are two other notable examples
among Sarajevo's 73 mosques, though
you may find some of the humbler little
places tucked away in the older suburbs
also appealing. The most important
Orthodox church was restored in the
1730s when its superb iconostasis was
added, though some of the fine collections
of icons go back to the 15th century. The
old but recently restored Jewish Syna-
gogue is a museum to the substantial
Jewish community that flourished here
from about 1500 onwards, as well as a
poignant record of the many thousands
liquidated during World War II.

The National Museum is a must if you
have any interest in the archaeological,
historical or ethnographic wealth of the
republic (there are good examples of
stećci, p. 55, in the courtyard). The Town
Museum is good of its kind, and Mlada
Bosna (Young Bosnia) Museum brings
together many documents, photographs
and personal belongings of the fervent
young revolutionaries whose activities
rocketed us all into World War I (p. 55).
Impressed on the pavement outside, the
footprints of Gavrilo Princip mark the
spot from which he shot Archduke Franz
Ferdinand in 1914. Finally, 18th-century
Moslem family life is well demonstrated
in Svrzo's House.

It is easy to get into the mountains from
the city. A road and cable car take you to
the nearest summit, Trebević (you might
like to pause at the new war memorial of
Vrace on the way). You can either go this
way, or via the pleasant little resort of
Pale, to **Jahorina** (36km/22mi), a well-
equipped winter and summer playground
that gained international status due to the
1984 Winter Olympics. The fully-
equipped winter sports centre on Bjelaš-
nica is another Olympic development.
Other mountain ranges which offer walk-

Princip Bridge, Sarajevo

Baščaršija, Sarajevo

Old water wheel near Trebinje

ing and some off-beat touring are Treskavica and Romanija.

Only 10km/6mi down the valley is **Ilidža** (tram service), a spa founded by the Romans and still active. Archduke Franz Ferdinand (p. 55) spent the last night of his life here. It's well worth the 3km/2mi walk or horse-and-buggy ride on to Vrelo Bosne, where the source of the Bosna river chatters out from many springs in the rock. Two other pleasant small spas in the area are **Kiseljak** (36km/22mi NW) and, in the hills beyond it, **Fojnica** (55km/34mi) whose Franciscan monastery has a well-arranged museum. *Zagreb 395km/247mi; Belgrade 321km/200mi.*

Travnik   H8

(pop. 64,100) The town was founded in the 15th century by the last Bosnian kings, but it was under Turkish rule that it gained importance. It was the seat of the Viziers of Bosnia from 1699–1851, a period immortalized by Nobel Prize winner Ivo Andrić in *The Bosnian Story*. Andrić's childhood home is now a museum. Despite a major fire at the turn of the century, the old part of Travnik on a fortress-crowned hill still exudes oriental charm and a number of important buildings survive from its heyday. The most

interesting are Hadži-Alibeg mosque and Šarena mosque. The latter, restored after a fire in 1815, has unusual decorated façades and a complex of small shops on the ground floor. The sarcophagi of some of the Travnik viziers and other notables of the time are masterpieces of 18th-century Islamic stone carving. *Sarajevo 126km/78mi.*

Trebinje   O10

(pop. 30,300) This little town offers the most accessible glimpse of 'oriental' Yugoslavia to holidaymakers on the nearby coast (Dubrovnik 32km/20mi). It stands on the river Trebišnjica, a curious waterway which disappears underground for a considerable distance through the surrounding karst, part of it reappearing near Dubrovnik as the Ombla. The beautiful late 16th-century bridge which crosses it is one of the town's fine sights. Others include the early 18th-century Osman Pasha mosque and an old Ottoman mansion, Begova kuća, housing a restaurant and theatre. A series of artificial lakes, fed by the Trebišnjica and other small rivers, now lies between Trebinje and **Bileća** (28km/17mi N), and the whole area is peppered with Illyrian tumuli and medieval cemeteries. *Sarajevo 204km/127mi.*

SERBIA
SRBIJA

Largest of the six republics, Serbia covers an area of 88,361sq km/34,116sq mi and extends from the fertile Danube plains to major mountain ranges in the south, the highest peak being Djeravica (2656m/8714ft) on the Albanian border. Serbia includes the two autonomous regions of Kosovo and Vojvodina and thus shelters the greatest number and diversity of minority nationalities in Yugoslavia. Of a total population of 9,300,000, only about two-thirds are Serbs.

Major archaeological finds from prehistory have occurred on Serbian soil, especially in the Danube basin, some giving their name to entire cultures such as Starčevo and Vinča (p. 7). The Danube itself formed the frontier of the Roman Empire and Serbia was then part of the Roman province of Pannonia. By the 7th century the Slavs had arrived and it was on Serbian and Montenegrin terrain that the first organized South Slav state was established, developing under the Nemanjić kings into an empire whose boundaries spread into Macedonia, Albania and half of Greece. Although the division of the Roman Empire in the late 4th century had left Serbia firmly in the Byzantine sphere of influence, the independent Serbian Orthodox church was founded early in the 13th century by St Sava, youngest brother of Stefan Nemanja, first of the powerful Nemanjić kings. During the following two centuries of Serbia's medieval power, many of the beautiful frescoed monasteries were built (see The Arts). Disastrous defeat by the Turks at the battle of Kosovo in 1389 marked the beginning of the end of Serb independence for nearly 500 years. During this period there were great migrations of Serbs, led by their religious leaders, especially in the late 17th and early 18th centuries. Many settled in what is now Vojvodina.

By this time, however, the tide was beginning to turn against Turkish rule. Prince Eugène of Savoy won major victories for the Austrians against the Turks and for a score of years parts of Serbia, including Belgrade, exchanged Turkish for Austrian rule, though to no great advantage. Early in the 19th century, growing nationalism exploded in a series of uprisings against the Turks, first under Djordje Petrović (known as Karadjordje or Black George) and then Miloš Obrenović. Serbia gained considerable autonomy in 1815 and was finally recognized as an independent state by the Congress of Berlin in 1878. Its future stability was not helped by a bitter feud between the Karadjordjević and Obrenović families that lasted for generations.

Serbia was a very different shape at the turn of the century. The capital Belgrade stood on its very frontiers, facing the uneasy lands – largely occupied by South Slavs – of the Habsburgs across the Danube and the Sava. Accused of complicity in the assassination of the Archduke Franz Ferdinand in Sarajevo in 1914 (p. 55), Serbia was presented with an impossible ultimatum by Austria, followed by a declaration of war which snowballed into the horrors of World War I. With Habsburg defeat, the Kingdom of the Serbs, Croats and Slovenes emerged on the map of Europe. The subsequent events are part of Yugoslavia's modern history (pp. 7–8).

Serbia is particularly rich in mineral resources and has many major industrial plants notably in the fields of mining, metallurgy, chemicals and heavy machinery. The agricultural Danubian plains of Vojvodina and adjoining regions are among the most fertile in Europe. Hydro-electric schemes on the Danube and massive irrigation systems between the Danube and the Tisa have virtually changed the face of many millions of hectares. Yet behind the modernization, the mountain ranges and their remote valleys are full of history, dotted with medieval monastic art treasures and still harbour a peasant way of life that is far removed from urban society. Bullock-, horse- and tractor-drawn traffic plods or rumbles through fields of sunflowers, peppers, tomatoes or pastureland beneath the mountains, and children and old folk, often in traditional dress, carve or spin as they watch over a couple of cows or a small flock of sheep. Many of the towns have

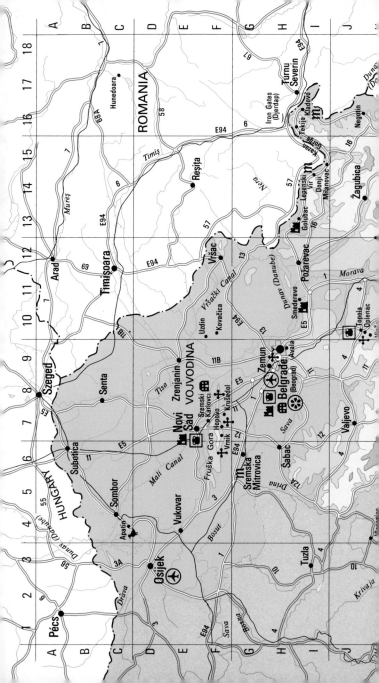

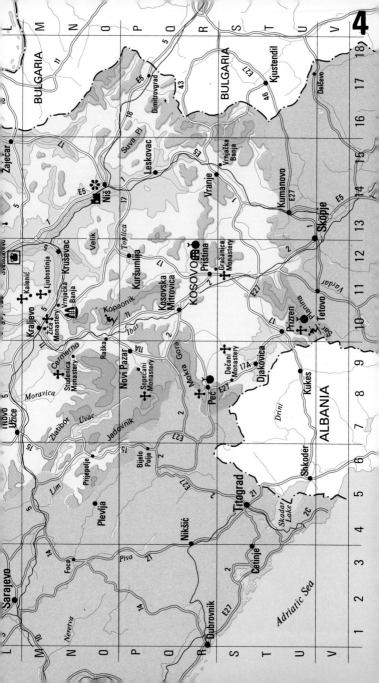

split personalities, the rather unbecoming new centres tacked on to the far more attractive if often crumbling older districts where artisans still beaver away in little workshops in the narrow alleys beneath the pencil shadows of minarets.

Note Because the monasteries are widely scattered, they are described in the gazetteer which follows under the places from which they are most easily reached. The most important are given under Kosovo, Kragujevac, Kraljevo and Novi Pazar.

Belgrade (Beograd)   H9

(pop. 1,455,000) Capital of Serbia as well as all Yugoslavia, Belgrade has a commanding position at the meeting of the Danube and Sava rivers. It was founded by the Celts, became the Roman *Singidunum*, was destroyed by the Huns, reconstructed by the Byzantines and finally became the 'white city' (Beli Grad) of the Slavs. Its ancient origins are not immediately obvious, for the city has been devastated many times by the movement of people and the ebb and flow of power politics. Poised on the brink of the Roman Empire, it was later overrun by the Turks, later still faced Habsburg might across the two rivers, and even later was shattered by bombardment in two World Wars. From the great fortress of Kalemegdan com-

manding the confluence, you get a very clear picture of Belgrade's situation as well as a magnificent view of the city.

The hub of present-day Belgrade is the main square, Trg Republike, bordered by the National Theatre, the National Museum (truly splendid collections from prehistory onwards) and the modern landmark of the Albanija building near which, in a pedestrian underpass, is the tourist information office. A little to the north east of the square lies Skadarlija, the one-time Bohemian district of Belgrade, now full of traditional restaurants, boutiques and galleries, and lively with crowds and street entertainment on summer evenings. North of the square is the older part of Belgrade. Sights here include the city's only surviving mosque (Bajrakli džamija), the Ethnographic Museum and the Frescoes Museum. The latter gives an excellent introduction to medieval monastic art, displaying reproductions of many of the best frescoes from Yugoslavia's medieval monasteries. A few blocks west is the 19th-century Orthodox Cathedral and its museum and, opposite, the Café of the Question Mark in a typical Serbian house of over one and a half centuries ago.

You are now close to the great park of Kalemegdan which contains the massive

City centre, Belgrade

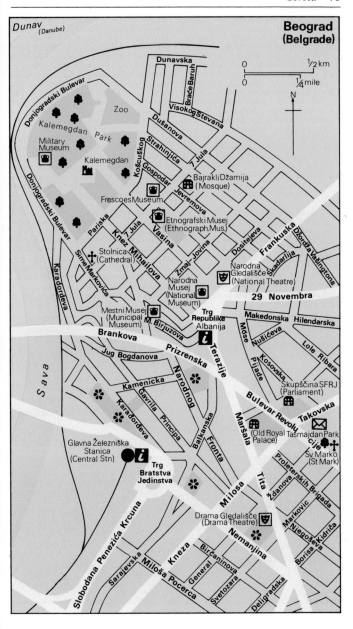

Dunav *(Danube)*

Beograd (Belgrade)

0 — 1/2 km
0 — 1/4 mile
N

Donjogradski Bulevar

Zoo

Kalemegdan Park

Military Museum

Kalemegdan

Dunavska

Brace Baruh

Visokog Stevana

Dušanova

Strahinjića

Košćuškog

Gospodar

Jula

Donjogradski Bulevar

Frescoes Museum

Bajrakli Džamija (Mosque)

Jevremova

Pariska

7 Jula

Vasina

Knez Mihailova

Sime Markovića

Karađorđeva

Stolnica (Cathedral)

Etnografski Musej (Ethnograph.Mus.)

Zmaj-Jovina

Dositejeva

Frankuska

Đorđa Vašingtona

Skadarlija

Narodna Gledališče (National Theatre)

Narodna Musej (National Museum)

29 Novembra

Mestni Musej (Municipal Museum)

M. Birjuzova

Trg Republike

Albanija

Makedonska

Hilendarska

Brankova

Sava

Jug Bogdanova

Prizrenska

Terazije

Mose

Nušićeva

Lole Ribara

Kosovska

Pijade

Skupščina SFRJ (Parliament)

Takovska

Kamenicka

Narodnog

Balkanska

Fronta

Maršala

Bulevar Revolu

(Old Royal Palace)

Tašmajdan Park

Sv Marko (St Mark)

Ždanova

Karađorđeva

Gavrila Principa

Glavna Železniška Stanica (Central Stn)

Trg Bratstva Jedinstva

Milosa

Tita

Prolererskih Brigada

Markovic

Drama Gledališče (Drama Theatre)

Nemanjina

Njegoševa

Kidriča

Borise

Slobodana Penezića Krcuna

Sarajevska

Miloša Pocerca

Kneza

Birčaninova

General

Svetozara

Deligradska

remains of the fortress originally founded by the Celts and enlarged and strengthened successively by the Romans, Serbs, Turks and Austrians. Most of what you see is Turkish and Austrian built, but much of the stonework is far older. The park also contains the outstanding Military Museum which relates to South Slav activities throughout the country and over the centuries. A number of sculptures in the park includes Meštrović's *Victory*. From the terraces of the fortress you look over to the white blocks of Novi Beograd (New Belgrade), built on what was swamp land until the 1950s and, beyond that, the little old satellite town of Zemun. Most of the big government and cultural institutions are in New Belgrade, along with the glossy new conference complex of the Sava Centre and the Modern Art Museum.

South of Trg Republike is the broad street of Terazije leading into Maršala Tita and Bulevar Revolucije with the imposing Federal Assembly building and, beyond it, in Tašmajdan Park, Sveti Marko, a copy of the church at Gračanica (p. 75). In a quiet suburb to the south of the centre lies the Tito Memorial Centre with his tomb in the house in which he lived and other museums associated with his life and times.

A popular local excursion is to wooded **Mount Avala** (20km/12mi S) with the Monument to an Unknown Soldier, supported by six statues in national dress, by Meštrović. A longer tour is the tiring but rewarding full-day hydrofoil trip to the Iron Gates through the spectacular **Kazan Gorges**. Another tour takes you to **Kovačica** and other villages in the Danubian plains to see the works of some of the naive painters (p. 77). One-day and longer excursions also take in some of the marvellous medieval monasteries. If you have a serious interest in archaeology, make enquiries about the latest excavations. New finds are forever turning up as foundations are laid for new developments in and around the city. See also **Kragujevac**, **Kraljevo**, **Smederevo**. *Zagreb 389km/243mi.*

Kazan Gorges   I15

The gorges can be seen on the hydrofoil excursion from Belgrade or, at more leisure, by road via **Smederevo** (p. 76) and the craggy medieval castle of **Golubac**. They are the culmination of a series of gorges (totalling about 100km/62mi in length) gouged out by the Danube on its passage through the Carpathians and arguably the most breathtaking stretch of the entire river which here forms the

Confluence of Danube and Sava rivers

Military Museum in Fort Kalemegdan

border with Romania. For centuries the turbulent waters presented a fearsome challenge to river travellers, but were at last tamed in 1972 with the completion of the hydro-electric dam and double locks of the **Iron Gates (Djerdap)**, a joint Yugoslav-Romanian venture. In the process the level of the river was substantially raised, drowning many villages which have since been rebuilt at a higher level. Half-submerged houses and trees punctuate the banks today.

The narrow gorges are interrupted by wider stretches of water and the rebuilt community of **Donji Milanovac** lies beside one such expanse. About 15km/9mi NW is **Lepenski Vir**, one of Europe's major archaeological sites. This Neolithic settlement has been carefully raised from its original site now under water. It dates back to up to 6000 BC and consists of several levels of houses, many of them trapezoidal in shape, thought possibly to be in imitation of the distinctive shape of the mountain on the opposite Romanian bank. Finds include some remarkable heads, sculpted from sandstone boulders, the earliest known sculptures to represent the human head life-size and larger. They are thought to be god-like guardians of the hearth, focal point of the houses excavated.

East of Donji Milanovac clear traces of a Roman military road, built partly on wooden supports jutting out from the cliff face, now lie, alas, under the raised waters. This road was an astonishing engineering feat and the original plaque commemorating its building has been resited above the present water level. This is Trajan's Tablet marking the completion of the road early in the 2nd century, though it was started in AD 33–34 in the reign of Tiberius. The plaque can only be seen from the river which here contracts to its narrowest point. In some of these narrow stretches the Danube is little more than 150m/500ft wide beneath towering cliffs of up to 700m/2300ft.

Tekija, another reconstructed community, lies 40km/25mi north east of Donji Milanovac and only a few miles west of the Iron Gates Dam, whose installations can be visited on conducted tours. The hydrofoil trip from Belgrade ends at **Kladovo**, 9km/6mi east of the dam, and a little beyond it are the very substantial traces of a huge Roman bridge built by Trajan in AD 103–105 in the great campaigns against Dacia (present-day Romania). Excavations have uncovered an extensive Roman settlement by the bridge. *Kladovo-Belgrade (via Smederevo) 253km/157mi.*

National Museum on Trg Republike, Belgrade

Priština

Prizren

Kosovo   R11

The autonomous region of Kosovo is
bordered by Macedonia, Albania and
Montenegro. Of its population of about 1½
million, over three-quarters are Albanian,
reflecting its turbulent history and ac-
counting for the very special ethnic nature
of the region. Much of the land is mountainous including the Šar-Planina and
Prokletije ranges with many peaks over
2000m/6560ft, but around the capital
Priština (pop. 211,000) are the plains on
which the momentous battle of Kosovo
was fought in 1389 (pp. 7, 75). Following
Serb defeat, the Turks ruled here right up
to the Balkan Wars of 1912 and 1913. It
was after a sizable exodus of Serbs in the
17th and 18th centuries that the region
was intensively settled by Albanians
(known as Šiptars or, in Albanian, Šqi-
petar). Nationalistic feelings have resulted
in considerable unrest, even leading to
federal intervention in recent years,
though àll is reported calm again.

Many Neolithic remains have been discovered but the overwhelming majority of
Kosovo's treasures date from medieval or
Turkish times. Most Kosovo towns have a
character all their own: a contrast of
indifferent modern building added on to a
jumble of houses and mosques along twisting streets where artisans perpetuate
traditional skills in tin, textiles or leather
in their little workshops. Often there are
brooks running through the streets and
there is much horse-drawn traffic with
jingling bells. Women in baggy pan-
taloons or men in striped woollen trousers
and white skull caps are still common
sights.

You can cover most of the sights of
Kosovo on a triangular route; at one point
stands Serbia's 'Canterbury', the Patriarchate of **Peć**. It crouches at the entrance to
Rugovska gorge where the seat of the
Serbian Orthodox Church was moved
(from Žiča) probably in the 13th century.
It was abolished after Turkish victory in
1389, restored in 1557 and survived for
two centuries as the heart of Serbian
spiritual life until abolished once again by
the Turks in 1766. But there remains a

Gračanica Monastery

fascinating complex of four churches featuring some magnificent frescoes of the Raška school (see The Arts). The Patriarchate is about 1½km/1m from the town of Peć, a jumble of new and old, part of it a maze of narrow streets, ramshackle houses and artisans' booths, dominated by the fine 15th-century Bajrakli mosque.

The imposing 14th-century monastery of **Dečani** lies 20km/12½mi south of Peć, off the main road at the entrance to another gorge. The mass of frescoes includes portraits of kings, nobles, saints and legendary and biblical scenes, showing crude attempts at perspective in a move away from the Byzantine formalism of the Raška school. **Djakovica**, 38km/24mi south of Peć, is worth visiting for its contrast of uninspired modern and jumbled old – the Turkish quarter has a dishevelled but considerable charm. **Prizren**, seat of the Nemanjić kings in the 13th and 14th centuries, 79km/49mi south east of Peć, is one of the most fascinating towns in the Balkans. The interiors of the houses, if you can manage to get a look in, are masterpieces of craftsmanship, from carved rose ceilings and bright carpets to the pewter and brass of everyday utensils. Of several interesting mosques and churches, don't miss at least Sv Bogorodica Ljeviška; its 14th-century frescoes, chipped away and plastered over by the Turks, have been restored. Near the ruined fortress of the Nemanjić kings on the hill south west of town is Sv Spas monastery founded by Tsar Dušan in 1348.

Kosovo's capital **Priština** lies 76km/47mi north east of Prizren and 81km/50mi east of Peć. It is mainly modern, but the old Turkish quarter has the usual dilapidated charm, a fine 15th-century mosque and *hamam* (baths), and lively market. Most important is the monastery of **Gračanica** (10km/6mi SE), a superb example of the Central or Kosmet school of the 14th century; it has a Nemanjić family tree. Only a few miles east of Priština is Kosovo Polje (Field of the Blackbirds) where the great battle of Kosovo took place in 1389, and where every spring a riot of red peonies are said to flower from the blood of the Serbian fallen. *Priština-Belgrade 377km/234mi.*

Kragujevac   L10

(pop. 164,800) This commercial town was briefly the capital of independent Serbia under Miloš Obrenović (p. 67) in the 19th century. It is also a living memorial to man's inhumanity for here, on 21 October, 1941, 7000 men and boys were shot in reprisal by the Germans. The memorial park on the outskirts has many fine monuments to this hideous event. About 40km/25mi east is **Svetozarevo** whose main claim for attention is its Gallery of Naive Paintings (p. 9), the biggest collection of its kind. Across the Morava river in the hills to the east are good examples of monasteries of the Morava school (see The Arts), notably at **Manasija** (25km/16mi NE of Svetozarevo) and **Ravanica** (29km/18mi E). North of Kragujevac is **Topola** (39km/24mi) where the home of the Karadjordjević family is a museum. On the hill of Oplenac above the town stands the family mausoleum. It was lavishly decorated in the 1920s with mosaics representing many of the frescoes from Serbia's monasteries. *Belgrade 120km/75mi.*

Kraljevo   M10

(pop. 121,600) This market town on the Ibar river is itself of no great interest, but there are many fine monasteries in the vicinity. Only a few miles south west is **Žiča**, site of the first Patriarchate of the Serbian Orthodox Church founded by Sv Sava and his brother King Stefan Nemanja. Much restored, it nevertheless retains frescoes from the 13th century onwards and has tremendous atmosphere, especially if your visit should coincide with a candle-lit mass. **Vrnjačka Banja** (25km/16mi SE) is Serbia's best known spa, a restful base from which to explore. There are two magnificent monasteries of the Morava school in the forested hills east of Kraljevo: **Ljubostinja** (35km/22mi) and, best of all, **Kalenić** (73km/45mi). *Belgrade 174km/108mi.*

Niš   O14

(pop. 230,700) At the junction of international through-routes to and from Romania, Bulgaria and Greece, Serbia's second largest and rather grimy city shows the marks of a long, long line of invaders and rulers. The two most important sights are Tvrdjava and Čele Kula. Just across the Nišava river, Tvrdjava is a huge fortification, mostly Turkish built in the late 17th century, now containing public gardens. Čele Kula (3km/2mi east of the centre) has a more grisly fascination for it means, and is, a tower of skulls, nearly 1000 of which were embedded in the stonework (only a few dozen have survived the elements and souvenir hunters) following a Serbian uprising that failed in 1809. *Belgrade 239km/148mi.*

Novi Pazar   P9

(pop. 74,000) An early capital of the Nemanjić kings and later a Turkish administrative centre, this is another hotchpotch of new and old, with plenty of the atmosphere of its Turkish past and a lively market. By the main road just north of town is ancient little Sv Petar, the oldest church in Serbia (early 10th century) where Stefan Nemanja was baptized, and, on a hill 2km/1mi west, the lonely 12th-century monastic remnants of Djurdjevi Stubovi.

There are two major monasteries in the area. **Sopoćani** (about 16km/10mi W) is magnificently placed at the head of a ravine. It was restored from a roofless ruin to preserve one of the finest achievements of the Raška school. Covering the west wall, the monumental fresco 'Dormition (death) of the Virgin' has a particularly grand serenity. The other monastery is **Studenica**, about 12km/7½mi up the Ibar gorge west from Ušće on the main road, and about halfway between Novi Pazar and Kraljevo. Again beautifully sited, it is the richest of all the Serbian monasteries, its three churches and monastic buildings protected by powerful walls, the whole restored in the late 16th century. The earliest and largest church, Sv Bogorodica, completed in 1191 with frescoes of the Raška school from 1209, has a marble exterior, a profusion of sculptures and the tomb of its founder Stefan Nemanja. The small white King's Church was founded by King Milutin in 1314. *Belgrade (via Kraljevo) 278km/174mi.*

Smederevo   I11

(pop. 107,300) One of the most imposing man-made sights on the Danube is the fortress of Smederevo, completed in 1430 (but later extended) as a bastion against the advancing Turks. It changed hands several times before the Turks finally held it in 1459 to remain there for the next 400 years, during which time an outer wall was added. It survived in a remarkable state of preservation until 1941 when it was used by the Germans as an ammunition dump which mysteriously exploded, blasting the fortress apart. Its ruined but massive walls and the remains of 25 towers rising out of the Danube are, however, a remarkable testimony to 15th-century building. *Belgrade 47km/29mi.*

Vojvodina   E8

The autonomous region of Vojvodina in the north of Serbia is bounded by Hungary, Romania, the Danube and the Sava rivers. Its huge agrarian plains are intersected by another great river, the Tisa, and an amazing network of canals making up the Danube-Tisa-Danube system that has revolutionized the productivity of this, Yugoslavia's 'granary'. The population of just over 2 million includes a miscellany of minority nationalities making it arguably the most polyglot corner of Europe with five languages in official use (Serbo-Croat, Hungarian, Romanian, Ruthenian and Slovak) and over a dozen others to be heard. For centuries part of Hungary, but ruled by Turkey for 150 years, this area witnessed some of Europe's most significant battles. One battle that changed the political face of Europe was the Turkish victory in 1526 at Mohacs, just over the border in Hungary. Later in Vojvodina, notably at Senta (Battle·of Zenta), the Turkish tide was reversed by Eugène of Savoy (p. 67). This led to the signing of the peace treaty between Austria and Turkey at Carlowitz (now Sremski Karlovci) in 1699, though Eugène had to trounce the Turks again, in 1717, at Peterwardein (Petrovaradin), the great fort facing Novi Sad across the Danube.

Novi Sad (pop. 214,000) is the capital of Vojvodina, a modern and highly civilized city with the excellent Vojvodina Museum and regional art gallery. It was known as the Serbian Athens as it became the hub of Serbian culture when large numbers of Serbs, fleeing Turkish-held areas further south, settled here in the late 17th and early 18th centuries. After the retreat of the Turks, the Habsburgs brought in large numbers of Germans, Slovaks, Hungarians and Ruthenians to settle the land and, in the process, added to Vojvodina's ethnic diversity.

The fortress of Petrovaradin is well worth visiting. It dates mainly from the 18th century and is built on eleven levels with 17km/11mi of underground passages and halls. Today it houses museums, a hotel and restaurant and gives splendid views over the river and Novi Sad. **Sremski Karlovci**, about 12km/7½mi south east, is today a sleepy wine-growing community by the Danube. A circular building commemorates the signing of the Austro-Turkish peace treaty in 1699, when the British were present as controllers. The town also became the seat of the Serbian Orthodox Church at the time of the Serb migrations and many monasteries were built, especially in the vine- and orchard-clothed hills of Fruška Gora that rise south of the Danube. Notable monasteries: **Krušedol, Hopovo, Vrnik**.

Subotica and **Sombor** are interesting towns in the north of Vojvodina, while the area round **Apatin** on the Danube is a little-known paradise for bird watchers. In the south, **Sremska Mitrovica** on the Sava river was the Roman *Sirmium* and offers substantial Roman remains. Some of the remote rural communities of Vojvodina, especially in the Banat district to the north of Belgrade, have produced a remarkable number of naive painters whose strong colours and simple forms vividly capture the rigours and relaxations of peasant life through the seasons. The artists of **Kovačica** (mainly Slovaks) and **Uzdin** (mainly Romanian women) are especially known and excursions are arranged from Belgrade. *Novi Sad-Belgrade 75km/47mi.*

Novi Sad

MONTENEGRO
CRNA GORA

The smallest of Yugoslavia's six republics, Montenegro covers an area of 13,812sq km/5335sq mi, most of it made up of extremely rugged mountains, the highest being the Durmitor massif (2522m/8274ft). The population is a little over half a million. The Yugoslavs call it Crna Gora, both versions of the name meaning 'Black Mountains' though, when the predominantly pale karst glints in the summer sun or is blanketed in winter snow, it seems rather a misnomer. In the south west, the wide expanses of Skadarsko jezero (Lake Skadar or Scutari, shared with Albania) are fed by the Morača river and its tributaries. The lake is separated by a range of low mountains from the narrow coastal strip with its string of popular resorts. Towards the border with Croatia, the mountains plunge almost sheer into the fjord-like and very beautiful Boka Kotorska (Gulf of Kotor). Equally dramatic are the many inland ravines created by rivers such as the Tara and the Morača.

Montenegrin history is as rugged as its topography. The earliest area of Slav settlement was Duklja, in the lowlands round the Zeta river, and in the Middle Ages it formed part of the expanding Serbian empire of the Nemanjić kings. Following the spread of Ottoman rule, after the Battle of Kosovo in 1389, many Montenegrins retired to their mountain fastnesses from which they waged protracted guerilla warfare against the Turks and those of their compatriots who had chosen conversion.

The clan feuds which raged over centuries were bitter and bloody and Montenegrin literature thunders with tales of fearsome deeds. As early as the late 15th century, Ivan Crnojević organized sufficient Montenegrin support to establish an independent principality centred on Cetinje. From the early 16th century it was governed by Orthodox Prince-Bishops, the most notable being those of the Petrović-Njegoš family. Among them, Petar II (who reigned 1830–50) was a man of great stature as well as a poet, and his *The Mountain Wreath* graphically describes the tragedy and humour of the Montenegrin dilemma. For the Turks were not the only enemy. The Venetians laid claim to part of the coast and, in turn, were in constant conflict with their Ottoman neighbours. Finally, from 1878–1918, the Gulf of Kotor became part of the package that went to the Habsburgs.

Nevertheless, 1878 was a significant date for, after the Congress of Berlin, Montenegro's sovereignty was internationally recognized and she at last won a stretch of coast around Bar and Ulcinj. In 1910, Nicolas I declared Montenegro a kingdom. Following World War II, this remained one of Yugoslavia's less-developed regions until the 1960s. Since then, a certain amount of industrialization, much improved communications and a surge of tourism have all wrought many changes. The wild, often remote mountain landscapes, however, remain totally unchanged if rather more accessible, and the fiercely independent and at times indolent Montenegrin temperament has not altered much either. It is definitely better not to assume that everything here will go according to plan! Many Montenegrins, however, have great culture and gentleness, and the unexpected can often be a big improvement on the scheduled.

In 1979, an earthquake inflicted severe damage especially along the coast. Most of the tourist amenities have been restored and expansion continues, but it will be some years before all the historical monuments are open to the public. Details are given, as far as they are available, in the gazetteer which follows. Communications are now good, with two major airports, at Tivat and Titograd, and easy access to that of Dubrovnik. The scenically superb rail route from Bar to Belgrade crosses the republic via Titograd. Main roads are well surfaced, and the rougher rides offered by minor roads are usually rewarded by grandiose landscapes and contact with a way of life still deeply rooted in old traditions.

Bar   H4
(pop. 32,500) Modern and expanding, Bar is Montenegro's only major seaport and its fairly recent rail link (above) with

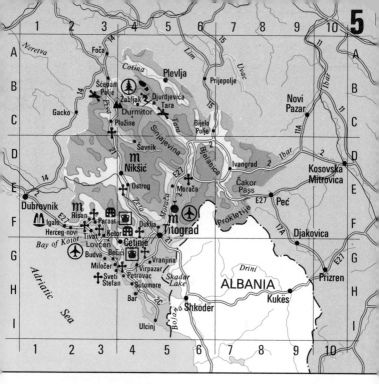

5

Belgrade is quite spectacular. A far more interesting community is **Stari** (Old) **Bar**, 3km/2mi inland, though it may still be closed following earthquake damage in 1979. Ruined medieval fortifications, churches and later Turkish buildings are scattered among twisted olive trees and wild flowers on the slopes of Mount Rumija. The pleasant resort of **Sutomore** is 8km/5mi north. Beyond it, the road passes beneath two craggy fortress ruins marking what was once the much-disputed border between Venetian- and Turkish-ruled territory. *Titograd 60km/ 37mi.*

Ferries: Bar is on express shipping routes linking main coastal centres Rijeka-Dubrovnik-(Greece); also Bar-Bari (Italy).

Boka Kotorska (see Kotor, Gulf of)

Budva   G3
(pop. 8600) From whichever direction you approach it, this compact little medieval walled town poised snugly on the shore makes a delightful picture. It

may still be closed to visitors following 1979 earthquake damage which seriously affected even those massive walls, originally built in the late 15th century and reconstructed in 1639. The Venetians ruled here for a long period and there are several old churches tucked away among the network of narrow streets. Outside the walls, the tourist facilities of modern Budva have been rebuilt or restored, and this is one of the most popular resorts of the whole coast. Most of the hotels and sports facilities are at **Bečići** (3km/2mi S) set amid fine gardens by a large beach of coarse sand. *Titograd 75km/46mi.*

Cetinje   G4
(pop. 20,200) This former royal capital of the one-time Kingdom of Montenegro has a sort of Ruritanian appeal. Its situation in a shallow bowl in the pale, arid karst mountains gives it exceedingly hot summers and stark cold winters. Even without the latest earthquake, which did a great deal of damage, the town seems subject to perpetual rebuilding, but the main monuments and museums should be restored by now.

As a royal city, albeit of toy-town pro-
portions, Cetinje had all the appropriate
trappings of palace, parliament and the
embassies and official residences of the
great powers of up to a hundred years ago-
British, American, Russian, French,
Austrian, Turkish and others. Most of the
latter now contain various institutions,
but the parliament·houses the History
Museum and Art Gallery. The house of
King Nicolas has been kept much as it was
at the time of his abdication in 1918 and
contains many gifts and other links with
foreign notables, including President
Roosevelt and the British royal family.
Across the road is the Biljarda, built as the
official residence by Njegoš Petar II in the
19th century, and so-called because of the
billiard table whose transport from the
coast over the then rugged track of the
Lovćen Pass was a major undertaking.
Looking rather like a fortified barracks,
the Biljarda now contains the interesting
Ethnographic Museum, Njegoš Museum,
Modern Art Gallery and a massive relief
map of the republic. Beyond it is the
Monastery of Cetinje, the late 18th-
century successor to the one founded, a
short distance away, by Ivan Crnojević in
1484, in which the first books to be printed
in a South Slav language were produced a
few years later. Nearby is the Tablja
Tower where the heads of slain Turks
were exhibited.

A modern, scenically splendid road
leads from Cetinje (in about 25km/16mi)
to the impressive mausoleum created by
Meštrović for Montenegro's most famous
ruler, the poet-prince Petar II Petrović-
Njegoš. It stands atop a 1574m/5164ft
ridge on Mount Lovćen and is usually
open 0800–1800. When you get to the end
of this long, winding road, there are still
some 400 steps to climb before you reach
the mausoleum itself. The views over
Cetinje and the Gulf of Kotor are stunning. *Titograd 63km/39mi.*

Peppers in the market, Cetinje

Old monastery now a museum, Cetinje

Montenegrin coastline

Old town, Budva

Mountainous landscape of Montenegro

Kotor, Gulf of   **F3**

Landscapes here match the fjords of Norway, as this contorted sea arm probes deep into the massive bulwarks of the Montenegrin mountains. It consists of a series of bays of the utmost complexity, linked by straits one of which can be crossed by ferry (Lepetane-Kamenari) at its narrowest point. A road follows most of the shoreline (total distance about 100km/62mi) linking a string of small communities, some of considerable age and some now developed into popular resorts.

Dramatic at any point, the scenery becomes increasingly spectacular as you progress inland towards the almost sheer wall of Mount Lovćen (1749m/5738ft). Clinging to its foot at the water's edge is the town of **Kotor** (pop. ·20,400) whose fortifications grasp the slopes above at incredible angles. The older walled part of Kotor is a real gem but, alas, much of it is still tottering from the latest earthquake. It will be some years before all is restored, though one of its finest buildings can be visited. This is the Cathedral, dating from 1116 but much reconstructed in the 17th and 18th centuries. Its numerous treasures include the carved Gothic ciborium and a

15th-century silver polyptych in bas-relief. There are several other old churches and some beautiful patrician houses, one of which, the 18th-century Grgurina Palace, houses a particularly fine Maritime Museum, largely devoted to the Seamen's Guild of the Gulf of Kotor whose records go right back to the 9th century.

The Gulf, very often part of the protracted tug-of-war between Venetian and Turk, was famous for its seafarers. In the little town of **Perast**, the 17th- and 18th-century buildings (one of them a naval school from 1698) are full of maritime ghosts who contributed to the greatness of the Venetian and, later, Russian fleets. Even more ancient is the community of **Risan** with some notable Roman mosaics from the 2nd century in a park just off the main road.

The most pleasant resort is **Herceg-novi**, with Riviera atmosphere, on the north shore, famed for its mimosa blossom in February and roses at other times. It too has ruined forts, one of them begun by the Spaniards in their brief occupation of 1538, but most of the remaining fortifications are Venetian or Turkish. A chief landmark is the

Town of Kotor below Mt Lovćen

17th-century Turkish clock tower. Herceg-novi's neighbour, **Igalo**, is known for its curative mud, and the two are linked by pleasant shoreside walks. **Tivat**, on the south shore, is a cargo port with a palm-lined promenade and an indifferent beach; the international airport is a few miles to the south.

It is well worth taking one of the many boat excursions round the Gulf, some of which include a picnic on one of the islets such as **Sveti Djordje** (St George) or **Gospa od Škrpjela**, both opposite Perast, and each bearing a church. The latter islet is artificial, built on to an underwater reef, stone by stone, in the 15th century. The interior paintings of the Baroque church are impressive and there are hundreds of votive plaques donated by sailors over the centuries.

From the sea, the view of the surrounding mountains soaring out of the deep blue waters and the pink-and-white villages strung along the shore is unforgettable. So is the breath-stopping drive on the serpentine road leading up the flanks of Mount Lovćen to Cetinje. It begins about 5km/3mi from Kotor and, as the climb progresses, the whole of the Gulf gradually unfolds below like a huge-scale map. *Herceg-novi-Dubrovnik 54km/34mi; Kotor-Titograd 88km/55mi.*

Nikšić E4

(pop. 72,300) This industrial town is a meeting point for several roads linking the coast and some of the finest mountain ranges of Montenegro and neighbouring Bosnia-Herzegovina. There are remains of old fortifications and, beside the church of Sv Petar, some Bogomil (p. 55) tombs. South east of town, the monastery of **Ostrog** (14km/9mi) crouches in a crack in a sheer rock face. Northwards a mountain road leads to Pivsko jezero (Piva lake), a great sinuous waterway created by one of Europe's highest dams. It passes **Piva Monastery** (16th century with frescoes) which was reconstructed near Plužine (71km/44mi) to preserve it from the rising waters. East of the lake rise the magnificent Durmitor mountains (see Žabljak). *Titograd 59km/37mi.*

Herceg-novi

Gulf of Kotor

Sveti Stefan

Sveti Stefan   H3

This half-abandoned fishing community on an islet just offshore was taken over for development as a tourist showplace in the 1950s. Most of the houses are from the 16th century, when the village was fortified, and each one has been tastefully adapted into first-class accommodation. There are small shops, a restaurant, a night club, and a causeway links the islet to the beach-lined mainland shore where there is a sports complex and open-air theatre. Close by on this shore is the small resort of **Miločer** which developed round the former summer palace of the Yugoslav royal family. The palace is now a hotel, and was a great favourite of President Tito. Another popular and pleasant resort, **Petrovac**, lies 10km/6mi south. On the way you pass a couple of the several monasteries with interesting frescoes along this coast: **Praskvica**, on the left almost above Miločer, and **Reževići**, on the right after about 7km/4mi. The monks seem delighted to show you round. From Petrovac it is 27km/17mi inland to Virpazar (p. 85). *Titograd 65km/40mi.*

Titograd   F5

(pop. 132,000) Formerly called Podgorica, the Montenegrin capital was rebuilt and renamed after almost total destruction in 1944. It is thus predominantly a very modern town, though a handful of interesting sights remain from its long

Fishing village on Lake Skadar

history. The oldest are on the north-west outskirts on the banks of the river Zeta where quite substantial remains – forum, baths, temples and early churches – of the original Roman town of *Dioclea* (now Duklja) can be seen. The ruined castle-fortress of the medieval Nemanjić kings of Serbia stands at the meeting of the Zeta and Morača rivers, and there are some old houses, the Ljubić mosque and Clock Tower from Turkish times.

The main road north from Titograd follows the very fine Morača valley, passing **Morača Monastery** (about 45km/28mi). This 13th-century complex is well worth visiting, not only for its lovely setting but for its interior frescoes, one of which portrays Elijah in the Wilderness and may well date back to 1252; the others are mainly from the 16th and 17th centuries. About halfway between Titograd and the coast (57km/35mi), the main road crosses a causeway through the strange landscapes created by Skadarsko jezero (Lake Skadar or Scutari), shared with neighbouring Albania. On its shores the fishing village of **Vranjina** and the small prettily-sited town of **Virpazar** both offer the possibility of fishing excursions in typical local flat-bottomed boats. Virpazar has a rather charming hotel in the local style, oddly named '13 July' to commemorate an uprising against the Germans in 1941. *Belgrade 450km/280mi.*

Ulcinj   I4

(pop. 21,500) The advent of tourism has modified the original oriental atmosphere of this little town, but it remains unusual. It is said to have been founded by Saracens, prior to nominal possession by Slav rulers. The Venetians then ruled for one and a half centuries, the Turks for three, during which time it became a launching pad for pirate attacks all over the Adriatic and Mediterranean, as well as a centre for traffic in African slaves. Traces of this mixed ancestry are occasionally noticeable

in the local population. The old part of town clambers about the slopes round a sandy bay, its silhouette punctuated by the remains of medieval fortifications, and there is a muddle of narrow streets, mosques, ruined churches and old houses, dilapidated partly by the 1979 earthquake, and partly because it seems to be the nature of the place.

Yugoslavia's greatest beach begins 4km/2½mi south east; this is **Velika Plaža** (Long Beach), stretching for 12km/7½mi almost to the Albanian border, with a cluster of modern hotels and other tourist amenities at its northern end. The greyish silky sands have an iodine content said to be highly beneficial to rheumatic sufferers, so it is quite common to see heads protruding while the rest of their owners bake gently under a covering of sand. Fishing on the nearby canal is still practised in the traditional way with extended nets lowered from the end of a pole. About 16km/10mi south of Ulcinj, the island of **Ada**, in the mouth of the river Bojana that forms the border with Albania, has

Market day in Ulcinj

become a particularly well-equipped naturist centre. *Titograd 115km/71mi.*

Žabljak   C4

At an altitude of 1450m/4757ft, Montenegro's best-equipped summer and winter mountain resort is set in the glorious Durmitor range (highest point Bobotov Kuk, 2522m/8274ft), now a national park. It's an area of sheep farmers and a way of life that has changed little once you get away from the tourist hotels. Marked trails make it easy for the energetic to explore spectacular surroundings that soar out of deeply-wooded ravines to high pasture and rock cliffs. In the vicinity there are eighteen lakes, with Crno jezero (Black Lake) a particular favourite, and fifteen peaks over 2000m/6560ft high. Of several grandiose ravines, the most famous is that of the Tara. Rafting trips lasting several days can be arranged (with advance notice) down its impatient waters from **Djurdjevića Tara** to **Šćepan Polje**. Overnights are spent in 'wild' campsites. This 60km/37mi-long canyon reaches to a maximum depth of 1300m/4265ft, in this respect second only to Colorado's Grand Canyon. *Titograd 144km/90mi.*

Valley of the Tara river

MACEDONIA
MAKEDONIJA

Yugoslavia's southernmost republic covers an area of 25,713sq km/9925sq mi, much of it mountainous (34 peaks over 2000m/6560ft). Most of its rivers drain via the main Vardar valley, through Greece, into the Aegean. Of the population of 1,900,000, 67 per cent are Macedonians speaking a South Slav language rather different from Serbo-Croat. Nearly 20 per cent are Albanians and there are substantial minorities of Turks, Serbs and Romanies.

The territory of the modern republic was, of course, part of the empire of Philip of Macedon and his son, Alexander the Great; later it was occupied by Rome. The original Romanized Illyrian and Celt inhabitants retreated to the mountains and were not absorbed during the Slav migrations; their descendants have probably survived in some degree as the Vlachs (Vlaši), mostly nomadic herdsmen. Much of Macedonia's early medieval history is shared with the adjoining areas of its immediate neighbours, Bulgaria, Greece and Albania. In the late 10th century Ohrid became the capital of the Bulgarian Tsar Samuilo (Samuel) who ruled over parts of these areas. By that time Ohrid was already an active centre for the teachings of Cyril and Methodius (p. 28). Samuilo's empire was brought to a ghastly end in 1014 when the Byzantine Basil II blinded 14,000 prisoners and sent them back as hideous warning against further dissidence. Samuilo died soon after.

Subsequently Macedonia came mainly under Byzantine control, then (from the late 14th century) under Turkish rule right up to the Balkan Wars of 1912–13. National awareness of Macedonian culture gained strength in the 19th century, leading to the formation of a revolutionary movement. The two World Wars, however, have left unsettled disputes over certain areas which now form part of Bulgaria or Greece.

Most of Macedonia's industries have developed since the 1950s, but it remains in many respects one of the poorest parts of Yugoslavia – and one of the most colourful. Almost every village has its own version of folk costume and culture, reflected in events which have become part of the tourist calendar, as well as in lively market days. The markets display the wide range of vegetables and fruit which with tobacco are Macedonia's main products. Horse- and bullock-drawn traffic plodding across a wide valley against a fine mountain backdrop, or a handful of livestock watering at a stream, watched over by young or old, are still essential parts of the country scene. And behind the sometimes ugly rash of post-war building, the older districts in communities have enormous charm beneath varying degrees of dishevelment. Magnificent medieval monasteries top the list of Macedonia's man-made heritage, but there are also fine buildings from the Turkish era.

Bitola   H4

(pop. 137,800) Macedonia's second biggest town lies close to the Greek border, 73km/45mi east of Ohrid. It is a pleasant place set in encircling hills, full of gardens, with the river Dragov chattering through it. Sv Dimitrije in the centre has a fine iconostasis and the old Turkish quarter offers lots of atmosphere, with its bazaar and covered market and several mosques, the best being Hajdargazi džamija. Only 1km/½mi south are the ruins of Roman **Heraclea**; once a major commercial centre on the Via Egnatia, it includes some stunning mosaics. *Skopje 159km/99mi.*

Debar   E1

(pop. 22,500) In the mountainous border country with Albania, 70km/43mi north west of Ohrid, this essentially Albanian town is stacked against the hillside above the Crni Drim river. Much of it has been rebuilt since an earthquake in 1967, but beneath the remaining dilapidation you can imagine how beautiful the typical houses once were, amidst their forest of minarets. About 40km/25mi north east, on the way to Skopje, lies the national park created round the town and artificial lake of **Mavrovo**. A turning to the right off this road leads to the monastery of **Sv Jovan Bigorski**, mainly from the 18th and 19th centuries, and worth a diversion for its secluded site clinging to steep crags, and its quite superb iconostasis. From the lake of Mavrovo a twisting mountain road brings you to **Galičnik**, an area famed for its master woodcarvers and its wedding customs (pp. 21, 23). *Skopje 141km/88 mi.*

Ohrid   H2

(pop. 64,300) Clustered on the north-east shore of Lake Ohrid at an altitude of 695m/2280ft, looking across to the blue mountains of the Albanian shore, this jewel of a place ranks, in its way, with Dubrovnik in historic, architectural and scenic interest. Its story is very much older, for Illyrians and Greeks were established nearby before it became an important centre on the Roman Via Egnatia. Soon after the arrival of the Slavs, it took on a major new role: in the late 9th century, Clement and Naum, disciples of Cyril and Methodius, established here the first Slav 'university' and cultural centre, teaching and spreading the new Slavonic alphabet (pp. 27–8). Within 100 years, Ohrid became the hub of the empire of Samuilo (Samuel) in constant conflict with the Byzantine empire which inflicted ferocious revenge (p. 87) in 1014. Yet, despite subsequent Byzantine rule, the Patriarchate of Ohrid retained considerable power, eventually proclaiming total independence from Constantinople; an independence that was abolished in 1767 and restored in 1967.

In the 12th–14th centuries monasteries and churches proliferated in and around Ohrid – about 40 survive in various stages of repair. Following the defeat of the Serbs in 1389, Ohrid fell to Turkey for over 500 years. Most of the churches were turned into mosques and their magnificent frescoes ravaged, but many have been restored using highly specialized techniques and infinite patience. From the Turkish period comes the extremely

charming (mainly 19th-century) domestic architecture, the bulging upper storeys of the houses at times almost touching across the narrow alleyways. Several of the houses contain different sections of the Ohrid Museum. Ohrid has a summerlong festival with much emphasis on folk costume and music, and a lively market.

The newer part of town sprawls back from the lake which, incidentally, harbours eighteen different kinds of fish, among them the unique *Ohridska belvica*, a kind of lake trout. The old town scrambles up and on to a hill topped by the ruins of Samuilo's castle. The oldest church, one of the most important in the whole country, is the Cathedral of Sv Sofije (from the 11th–14th centuries on earlier foundations), later turned into a mosque. Many of the restored frescoes are from the 11th century. Sv Kliment, above the town, is an ornamented brick church from the late 13th century, with a battery of frescoes which includes some of the earliest works of Mihajlo and Eutihije (see The Arts). This was the main Orthodox sanctuary during Turkish rule; its frescoes (now restored) suffered from the smoke of generations of candles rather than Turkish iconoclasm.

West of the old town and below the castle, the tiny church of Sv Jovan Bogoslov is gloriously perched above the lake near the village of Kaneo. Between this church and the castle are the interesting and well-organized ruins of Sv Pantalejmon, the monastery and 'university' founded by Clement in 893; the Turks turned it into a mosque, now without roof or minaret, but traces of the original foundations can still be seen and it is an intensely peaceful spot. Of the many other churches, of particular interest are Sv Bogorodica Bolnička (frescoes and rich iconostasis) and Sv Nikola Bolnička (good frescoes).

Sv Jovan Bogoslov near Kaneo

Beach at St Naum on Lake Ohrid

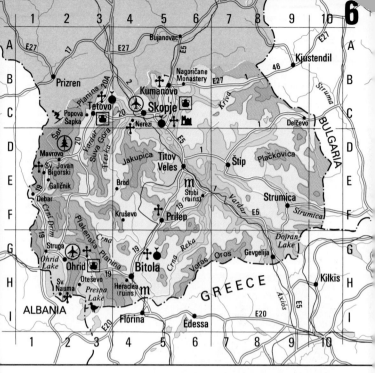

6

A pleasant excursion by boat or road is to the monastery of **St Naum** (Svetog Nauma, 29km/18mi S), on a rock promontory by the lake almost on the Albanian border. The present church dates from the 14th–17th centuries, but traces of the original 10th-century church can be seen, as well as the tomb of St Naum. **Struga** (14km/9mi NW) is another attractive place, with a poetry festival (p. 24) Beyond the hills to the south east, about 50km/31mi by road, lies the wilder and even larger lake of **Prespa** (shared with Greece and Albania), famed for its fish

Monastery of St Naum, Lake Ohrid

and also the haunt of any ornithologists who may be about (there are pelicans here). There's a modern tourist complex at **Oteševo** on the north-west shore. *Skopje 180km/112mi.*

Prilep   F5

(pop. 99,900) A tobacco-producing centre set among arid hills, this is another town full of its Turkish past, worth a leisurely wander round the mosques and churches and the bazaar area. On a rocky hill above stand the craggy ruins of the castle of Marko Kraljević, one of Yugoslavia's most colourful characters – a kind of 14th-century Serbian Robin Hood whose legendary (rather than historical) heroic deeds against the Turks are the theme of innumerable ballads (p. 9). The monasteries of Sv Arhangel and Sv Nikola and the early 14th-century church complex of Sv Dimitrije are all worth attention. In rugged mountain country (30km/19mi W) is the interesting small town of **Kruševo** where a rebellion in 1903 led to the proclamation of the first Macedonian republic; it lasted twelve days. *Skopje 134km/83mi.*

Skopje (Skoplje)   C4

(pop. 503,000) The Macedonian capital straddles the upper Vardar river, surrounded by mountains, on the main road through to Greece. Much of its modern aspect dates from rebuilding after a devastating earthquake in July 1963, which brought assistance flooding in from all over the world. Happily, quite a few of the monuments which mark its turbulent history survived or have been restored. Founded, probably by Justinian, on the site of *Skupi*, the capital of the Illyrian province of Dardania, Skopje came by turn under Byzantine, Macedonian and Bulgarian rule until it became part of medieval Serbia, eventually sharing in the same defeat by the Turks who ruled here for over 500 years. Most of the monuments are from that period.

Heart of the new city is Trg Maršala Tita, completely rebuilt since the earthquake. The fine Ethnographic Museum is here and, from the square, Maršala Tita street leads to the new and old railway stations, the latter left in its ruined state with its clock stopped at the ill-fated moment when the earthquake struck. From Trg Maršala Tita you can cross the Vardar by the narrow 15th-century stone bridge to the older and more interesting part of town. Major sights are: Daut Pasha's Hamam (1466) with thirteen different cupolas, now restored and containing an excellent art museum; 17th-century Sv Spas (St Saviour) with a superb iconostasis, completed 1825; Kale Fortress dominating the town, mainly from Turkish times but incorporating 6th-century stonework; late 15th-century Mustapha Pasha mosque, the finest in town; 16th-century Kuršumli Han, now housing the Archaeological Museum; the twisting little streets that harbour innumerable artisan workshops, and the very big open-air market of Bit Pazar.

Skopje's surroundings are dotted with old monasteries. The most important, perched on Vodno mountain with a fabulous view over the city, is 12th-century Sv

Old Turkish quarter, Skopje

Bridge over Vardar river, Skopje

Pantalejmon at **Nerezi** (5km/3mi) with some original frescoes. The monks' quarters are now a restaurant. **Kumanovo** (35km/22mi NE) is another centre for medieval monuments. The most famous is the graceful little 14th-century church of **Staro Nagoričane** and its original and splendidly vigorous frescoes (about 20km/12mi NE of Skopje). *Belgrade 437km/273mi.*

Tetovo C3

(pop. 62,400) A major tobacco town, Tetovo has enormous charm once you get away from the modern centre. There are gardens and streams and the pinks and blues of old houses with studded doors and grilled apertures where, in the late summer, you are likely to see women crouching at work in the verandahs, grading and wiring tobacco leaves. Šarena Džamija or the 'Coloured Mosque', with its decorated façades, is an attractive building, but the most interesting group, near a great Moslem cemetery on the south-west side of town, is the Tekija or Whirling Dervish Monastery complete with harem quarters, a unique survivor of its kind in Yugoslavia, and now containing the Town Museum. The town backs on to the lower slopes of Šar-Planina and a cable car leads to the developing winter sports resort of **Popova Šapka** (1875m/6151ft). *Skopje 44km/27mi.*

Titov Veles E6

(pop. 64,900) This agricultural and industrial centre in the Vardar valley has few traces of its long history, but it has a pleasant situation, terraced on either side of the river. Near the main road, about 28km/17mi south east, beyond Gradska, are substantial Roman ruins of **Stobi** destroyed in an earthquake in 518, now scattered about the sunbaked countryside. Remains include an amphitheatre, several palaces and churches, and a public bath. Most of the best finds have been removed to museums in Skopje and Belgrade. *Skopje 52km/32mi.*

Monastery of Sv Pantalejmon at Nerezi

INDEX

All main entries are printed in heavy type. Map references are also printed in heavy type.
The map page number precedes the grid reference.